The Fire Next Time

with Connections

The Fire Next Time

James Baldwin

with
Connections

HOLT, RINEHART AND WINSTON
Harcourt Brace & Company

Austin • New York • Orlando • Atlanta • San Francisco
Boston • Dallas • Toronto • London

For permission to reprint copyrighted material, grateful acknowledgment is made to the
following sources:

James Baldwin Estate: The Fire Next Time by James Baldwin. Copyright © 1962, 1963 and renewed
© 1990 by James Baldwin. Published by Vintage Books. "Down At the Cross" was originally
published under the title "Letter from a Region in My Mind" in the *The New Yorker.* "My Dungeon
Shook" originally appeared in *The Progressive.*

Don Congdon Associates, Inc. From "Jimmy in the House" by William Styron from *James Baldwin:
The Legacy,* edited by Quincy Troupe. Copyright © 1989 by William Styron. Published by Simon &
Schuster. *Henry Louis Gates, Jr., c/o Janklow & Nesbit Associates:* Adapted from "After the
Revolution" by Henry Louis Gates, Jr. Originally published in *The New Yorker.* Copyright © 1996 by
Henry Louis Gates, Jr. *International Creative Management, Inc.:* "A Knowing So Deep" by Toni
Morrison from *Essays by Contemporary American Women,* edited by Wendy Martin. Copyright ©
1985 by Toni Morrison. *Alfred A. Knopf, a Division of Random House, Inc.* "Passing" from *The
Ways of White Folks* by Langston Hughes. Copyright 1934 and renewed © 1962 by Langston Hughes.
Pathfinder Press: Interview by Les Crane with Malcolm X, "Whatever Is Necessary to Protect
Ourselves," December 27, 1964, from *Malcolm X: The Last Speeches,* edited by Bruce Perry.
Copyright © 1989 by Betty Shabazz, Bruce Perry, and Pathfinder Press. *The Peters Fraser and
Dunlop Group Ltd., on behalf of the Estate of V. S. Pritchett:* "The Saint" from *Complete Collected
Stories* by V. S. Pritchett. Copyright 1945, © 1990 by V. S. Pritchett. *Sanga Music, Inc.:* Lyrics to
"Burn, Baby, Burn" by Jimmy Collier. Copyright © 1966 by Sanga Music, Inc. All rights reserved.
Sing Out Corp.: Introduction by Jimmy Collier to *Sing for Freedom: The Story of the Civil Rights
Movement Through Its Songs,* compiled and edited by Guy and Candie Carawan. Copyright © 1990,
1992 by Sing Out Corporation.

Cover: Victoria Smith, HRW photo

Printed in the United States of America

ISBN 0-03-055442-X

18 803 15

4500563511

for James
James
Luc James

"God gave Noah the rainbow sign,
No more water, the fire next time!"

Contents

MY DUNGEON SHOOK

*Letter to My Nephew
on the One Hundredth Anniversary of
the Emancipation*

Dear James:

I HAVE BEGUN this letter five times and torn it up five times. I keep seeing your face, which is also the face of your father and my brother. Like him, you are tough, dark, vulnerable, moody—

with a very definite tendency to sound truculent because you want no one to think you are soft. You may be like your grandfather in this, I don't know, but certainly both you and your father resemble him very much physically. Well, he is dead, he never saw you, and he had a terrible life; he was defeated long before he died because, at the bottom of his heart, he really believed what white people said about him. This is one of the reasons that he became so holy. I am sure that your father has told you something about all that. Neither you nor your father exhibit any tendency towards holiness: you really *are* of another era, part of what happened when the Negro left the land and came into what the late E. Franklin Frazier called "the cities of destruction." You can only be destroyed by believing that you really are what the white world calls a *nigger*. I tell you this because I love you, and please don't you ever forget it.

I have known both of you all your lives, have carried your Daddy in my arms and on my shoulders, kissed and spanked him and watched him learn to walk. I don't know if you've known anybody from that far back; if you've loved anybody that long, first as an infant, then as a child, then as a man, you gain a strange perspective on time and human pain and effort. Other people cannot see what I see whenever I look into your father's face, for behind your father's face as it is today are all those other faces which were his. Let him laugh and I see a cellar your father does not remember and a house he does not remember and I hear in his present laughter his laughter as a child. Let him curse and I remember him falling down the cellar steps, and howling, and I remember, with pain, his tears, which my hand or your grandmother's so easily wiped away. But no one's hand can wipe away those tears he sheds invisibly today, which one hears in his laughter and in his speech and in his songs. I know what the world has done to my brother and how narrowly he has survived it. And I know, which is much worse, and this is the crime of which I accuse my country and my countrymen, and for which neither I nor time nor history will ever forgive them, that they have destroyed and are destroying hundreds of thousands of lives and do not know it and do not want to know it. One can be, indeed one must strive to become, tough and philosophical concerning destruction and death, for this is what most of mankind has been best at since we have heard of man. (But remember: *most* of mankind is not *all* of mankind.) But it is not permissible that the authors of devastation should also be innocent. It is the innocence which constitutes the crime.

Now, my dear namesake, these innocent and well-meaning people, your countrymen, have caused you to be born under conditions not very far removed from those described for us by Charles Dickens in the London of more than a hundred years ago. (I hear the chorus of the innocents screaming, "No! This is not true! How *bitter* you are!"—but I am writing this letter to *you,* to try to tell you something about how to handle *them,* for most of them do not yet really know that you exist. I *know* the conditions under which you were born, for I was there. Your countrymen were *not* there, and haven't made it yet. Your grandmother was also there, and no one has ever accused her of being bitter. I suggest that the innocents check with her. She isn't hard to find. Your countrymen don't know that *she* exists, either, though she has been working for them all their lives.)

Well, you were born, here you came, something like fifteen years ago; and though your father and mother and grandmother, looking about the streets through which they were carrying you, staring at the walls into which they brought you, had every reason to be heavyhearted, yet they were not. For here you were, Big James, named for me—you were a big baby, I was not—here you were: to be loved. To be loved, baby, hard, at once, and forever, to strengthen you against the loveless world. Remember that: I know how black it looks today, for you. It looked bad that day, too, yes, we were trembling. We have not stopped trembling yet, but if we had not loved each other none of us would have survived. And now you must survive because we love you, and for the sake of your children and your children's children.

This innocent country set you down in a ghetto in which, in fact, it intended that you should perish. Let me spell out precisely what I mean by that, for the heart of the matter is here, and the root of my dispute with my country. You were born where you were born and faced the future that you faced because you were black and *for no other reason*. The limits of your ambition were, thus, expected to be set forever. You were born into a society which spelled out with brutal clarity, and in as many ways as possible, that you were a worthless human being. You were not expected to aspire to excellence: you were expected to make peace with mediocrity. Wherever you have turned, James, in your short time on this earth, you have been told where you could go and what you could do (and *how* you could do it) and where you could live and whom you could marry. I know your country-men do not agree with me about this, and I hear them saying, "You exaggerate." They do not know Harlem, and I do. So do you. Take no one's word for anything, including mine—but trust your experience. Know whence you came. If you know whence you came, there is really no limit to where you can go. The details and symbols of your life have been deliberately constructed to make you believe what white people say about you. Please try to remember that what they believe, as well as what they do and cause you to endure, does not testify to your inferiority but to their inhumanity and fear. Please try to be clear, dear James, through the storm which rages about your youthful head today, about the reality which lies behind the words *acceptance* and *integration*. There is no reason for you to try to become like white people and there is no basis whatever for their impertinent assumption that *they* must accept *you*. The really terrible thing, old buddy, is that *you* must accept *them*. And I mean that very seriously. You must accept them and accept them with love. For these innocent people have no other hope. They are, in effect, still trapped in a history which they do not understand; and until they understand it, they cannot be released from it. They have had to believe for many years, and for innumerable reasons, that black men are inferior to white men. Many of them, indeed, know better, but, as you will discover, people find it very difficult to act on what they know. To act is to be committed, and to be committed is to be in danger. In this case, the danger, in the minds of most white Americans, is the loss of their identity. Try to imagine how you would feel if you woke up one morning to find the sun shining and all the stars aflame. You would be frightened because it is out of the order of nature. Any upheaval in the universe is terrifying because it so profoundly attacks one's sense of one's own reality. Well, the black man has functioned in the white man's world as a fixed star, as an immovable pillar: and as he moves out of his place, heaven and earth are shaken to their foundations. You, don't be afraid. I said that it was intended that you should perish in the ghetto, perish by never being allowed to go behind the white man's definitions, by never being allowed to spell your proper name. You have, and many of us have, defeated this intention; and, by a terrible law, a terrible paradox, those innocents who believed that your imprisonment made them safe are losing their grasp of reality. But these men are your brothers—your lost, younger brothers. And if the word *integration* means anything, this is what it means: that we, with love, shall force our brothers to see themselves as they are, to cease fleeing from reality and begin to change it. For this is your home, my friend, do not be driven from it; great men have done great things here, and will again, and we can make America what America must become. It will be hard, James, but you come from sturdy, peasant stock, men who picked cotton and dammed rivers and built railroads, and, in the teeth of the most terrifying odds, achieved an unassailable and monumental dignity. You come from a long line of great poets, some of the greatest poets since Homer. One of them said, *The very time I thought I was lost, My dungeon shook and my chains fell off.*

You know, and I know, that the country is celebrating one hundred years of freedom one hundred years too soon. We cannot be free until they are free. God bless you, James, and Godspeed.

Your uncle,
James

DOWN
AT THE
CROSS

Letter from a Region in My Mind

Take up the White Man's burden—
Ye dare not stoop to less—
Nor call too loud on Freedom
To cloak your weariness;
By all ye cry or whisper,
By all ye leave or do,
The silent, sullen peoples
Shall weigh your Gods and you.

—Kipling

Down at the cross where my Saviour died,
Down where for cleansing from sin I cried,
There to my heart was the blood applied,
Singing glory to His name!

—Hymn

I UNDERWENT, during the summer that I became fourteen, a prolonged religious crisis. I use the word "religious" in the common, and arbitrary, sense, meaning that I then discovered

God, His saints and angels, and His blazing Hell. And since I had been born in a Christian nation, I accepted this Deity as the only one. I supposed Him to exist only within the walls of a church—in fact, of *our* church—and I also supposed that God and safety were synonymous. The word "safety" brings us to the real meaning of the word "religious" as we use it. Therefore, to state it in another, more accurate way, I became, during my fourteenth year, for the first time in my life, afraid—afraid of the evil within me and afraid of the evil without. What I saw around me that summer in Harlem was what I had always seen; nothing had changed. But now, without any warning, the whores and pimps and racketeers on the Avenue had become a personal menace. It had not before occurred to me that I could become one of them, but now I realized that we had been produced by the same circumstances. Many of my comrades were clearly headed for the Avenue, and my father said that I was headed that way, too. My friends began to drink and smoke, and embarked—at first avid, then groaning—on their sexual careers. Girls, only slightly older than I was, who sang in the choir or taught Sunday school, the children of holy parents, underwent, before my eyes, their incredible metamorphosis, of which the most bewildering aspect was not their budding breasts or their rounding behinds but something deeper and more subtle, in their eyes, their heat, their odor, and the inflection of their voices. Like the strangers on the Avenue, they became, in the twinkling of an eye, unutterably different and fantastically *present*. Owing to the way I had been raised, the abrupt discomfort that all this aroused in me and the fact that I had no idea what my voice or my mind or my body was likely to do next caused me to consider myself one of the most depraved people on earth. Matters were not helped by the fact that these holy girls seemed rather to enjoy my terrified lapses, our grim, guilty, tormented experiments, which were at once as chill and joyless as the Russian steppes and hotter, by far, than all the fires of Hell.

Yet there was something deeper than these changes, and less definable, that frightened me. It was real in both the boys and the girls, but it was, somehow, more vivid in the boys. In the case of the girls, one watched them turning into matrons before they had become women. They began to manifest a curious and really rather terrifying single-mindedness. It is hard to say exactly how this was conveyed: something implacable in the set of the lips, something farseeing (seeing what?) in the eyes, some new and crushing determination in the

17

walk, something peremptory in the voice. They did not tease us, the boys, any more; they reprimanded us sharply, saying, "You better be thinking about your soul!" For the girls also saw the evidence on the Avenue, knew what the price would be, for them, of one misstep, knew that they had to be protected and that we were the only protection there was. They understood that they must act as God's decoys, saving the souls of the boys for Jesus and binding the bodies of the boys in marriage. For this was the beginning of our burning time, and "It is better," said St. Paul—who elsewhere, with a most unusual and stunning exactness, described himself as a "wretched man"—"to marry than to burn." And I began to feel in the boys a curious, wary, bewildered despair, as though they were now settling in for the long, hard winter of life. I did not know then what it was that I was reacting to; I put it to myself that they were letting themselves go. In the same way that the girls were destined to gain as much weight as their mothers, the boys, it was clear, would rise no higher than their fathers. School began to reveal itself, therefore, as a child's game that one could not win, and boys dropped out of school and went to work. My father wanted me to do the same. I refused, even though I no longer had any illusions about what an

education could do for me; I had already encountered too many college-graduate handymen.
My friends were now "downtown," busy, as they
put it, "fighting the man." They began to care less
about the way they looked, the way they dressed,
the things they did; presently, one found them in
twos and threes and fours, in a hallway, sharing a
jug of wine or a bottle of whiskey, talking, cursing,
fighting, sometimes weeping: lost, and unable to
say what it was that oppressed them, except that
they knew it was "the man"—the white man. And
there seemed to be no way whatever to remove
this cloud that stood between them and the sun,
between them and love and life and power, between them and whatever it was that they wanted.
One did not have to be very bright to realize how
little one could do to change one's situation; one
did not have to be abnormally sensitive to be worn
down to a cutting edge by the incessant and gratuitous humiliation and danger one encountered
every working day, all day long. The humiliation
did not apply merely to working days, or workers;
I was thirteen and was crossing Fifth Avenue on
my way to the Forty-second Street library, and
the cop in the middle of the street muttered as I
passed him, "Why don't you niggers stay uptown
where you belong?" When I was ten, and didn't

look, certainly, any older, two policemen amused themselves with me by frisking me, making comic (and terrifying) speculations concerning my ancestry and probable sexual prowess, and for good measure, leaving me flat on my back in one of Harlem's empty lots. Just before and then during the Second World War, many of my friends fled into the service, all to be changed there, and rarely for the better, many to be ruined, and many to die. Others fled to other states and cities—that is, to other ghettos. Some went on wine or whiskey or the needle, and are still on it. And others, like me, fled into the church.

For the wages of sin were visible everywhere, in every wine-stained and urine-splashed hallway, in every clanging ambulance bell, in every scar on the faces of the pimps and their whores, in every helpless, newborn baby being brought into this danger, in every knife and pistol fight on the Avenue, and in every disastrous bulletin: a cousin, mother of six, suddenly gone mad, the children parcelled out here and there; an indestructible aunt rewarded for years of hard labor by a slow, agonizing death in a terrible small room; someone's bright son blown into eternity by his own hand; another turned robber and carried off to jail. It was a summer of dreadful speculations and discoveries, of which these were not the worst. Crime became real, for example—for the first time—not as *a* possibility but as *the* possibility. One would never defeat one's circumstances by working and saving one's pennies; one would never, by working, acquire that many pennies, and, besides, the social treatment accorded even the most successful Negroes proved that one needed, in order to be free, something more than a bank account. One needed a handle, a lever, a means of inspiring fear. It was absolutely clear that the police would whip you and take you in as long as they could get away with it, and that everyone else—housewives, taxi-drivers, elevator boys, dishwashers, bartenders, lawyers, judges, doctors, and grocers—would never, by the operation of any generous human feeling, cease to use you as an outlet for his frustrations and hostilities. Neither civilized reason nor Christian love would cause any of those people to treat you as they presumably wanted to be treated; only the fear of your power to retaliate would cause them to do that, or to seem to do it, which was (and is) good enough. There appears to be a vast amount of confusion on this point, but I do not know many Negroes who are eager to be "accepted" by white people, still less to be loved by them; they, the blacks, simply don't wish to be beaten over the head by the whites every instant of our brief passage on this planet. White people in this country will have quite enough to do in learning how to accept and love themselves and each other, and when they have achieved this— which will not be tomorrow and may very well be never—the Negro problem will no longer exist, for it will no longer be needed.

People more advantageously placed than we in Harlem were, and are, will no doubt find the psychology and the view of human nature sketched above dismal and shocking in the extreme. But the Negro's experience of the white world cannot possibly create in him any respect for the standards by which the white world claims to live. His own condition is overwhelming proof that white people do not live by these standards. Negro servants have been smuggling odds and ends out of white homes for generations, and white people have been delighted to have them do it, because it has assuaged a dim guilt and testified to the intrinsic superiority of white people. Even the most doltish and servile Negro could scarcely fail to be impressed by the disparity between his situation and that of the people for whom he worked; Negroes who were neither doltish nor servile did not feel that they were doing anything wrong when they robbed white people. In spite of the Puritan-Yankee equation of virtue with well-being, Negroes had excellent reasons for doubting that money was made or kept by any very striking adherence to the Christian virtues; it certainly did not work that way for black Christians. In any case, white people, who had robbed black people of their liberty and who profited by this theft every hour that they lived, had no moral ground on which to stand. They had the judges, the juries, the shotguns, the law—in a word, power. But it was a criminal power, to be feared but not respected, and to be outwitted in any way whatever. And those virtues preached but not practiced by the white world were merely another means of holding Negroes in subjection.

It turned out, then, that summer, that the moral barriers that I had supposed to exist between me and the dangers of a criminal career were so tenuous as to be nearly nonexistent. I certainly could not discover any principled reason for not becoming a criminal, and it is not my poor, God-fearing parents who are to be indicted for the lack but this society. I was icily determined—more determined, really, than I then knew—never to make my peace with the ghetto but to die and go to Hell before I would let any white man spit on me, before I would accept my "place" in this republic. I did not intend to allow the white people of this country to tell me who I was, and limit me that way, and polish me off that way. And yet, of course, at the same time, I *was* being spat on and defined and described and limited, and could have been polished off with no effort whatever. Every Negro boy—in my situation during those years, at least—who reaches this point realizes, at once, profoundly, because he wants to live, that he stands in great peril and must find, with speed, a "thing," a gimmick, to lift him out, to start him on his way. *And it does not matter what the gimmick is.* It was this last realization that terrified me and—since it revealed that the door opened on so many dangers—helped to hurl me into the church. And, by an unforeseeable paradox, it was my career in the church that turned out, precisely, to be my gimmick.

For when I tried to assess my capabilities, I realized that I had almost none. In order to achieve the life I wanted, I had been dealt, it seemed to me, the worst possible hand. I could not become a prize-fighter—many of us tried but very few succeeded. I could not sing. I could not dance. I had been well conditioned by the world in which I grew up, so I did not yet dare take the idea of becoming a writer seriously. The only other possibility seemed to involve my becoming one of the sordid people on the Avenue, who were not really as sordid as I then imagined but who frightened me terribly, both because I did not want to live that life and because of what they made me feel. Everything inflamed me, and that was bad enough, but I myself had also become a source of fire and temptation. I had been far too well raised, alas, to suppose that any of the extremely explicit overtures made to me that summer, sometimes by boys and girls but also, more alarmingly, by older men and women, had anything to do with my attractiveness. On the contrary, since the Harlem idea of seduction is, to put it mildly, blunt, whatever these people saw in me merely confirmed my sense of my depravity.

It is certainly sad that the awakening of one's senses should lead to such a merciless judgment of oneself—to say nothing of the time and anguish one spends in the effort to arrive at any other—but it is also inevitable that a literal attempt to mortify the flesh should be made among black people like those with whom I grew up. Negroes in this country—and Negroes do not, strictly or legally speaking, exist in any other—are taught really to despise themselves from the moment their eyes open on the world. This world is white and they are black. White people hold the power, which means that they are superior to blacks (intrinsically, that is: God decreed it so), and the world has innumerable ways of making this difference known and felt and feared. Long before the Negro child perceives this difference, and even longer before he understands it, he has begun to react to it, he has begun to be controlled by it. Every effort made by the child's elders to prepare him for a fate from which they cannot protect him causes him secretly, in terror, to begin to await, without knowing that he is doing so, his mysterious and inexorable punishment. He must be "good" not only in order to please his parents and not only to avoid being punished by them; behind their authority stands another, nameless and impersonal, infinitely harder to please, and bottomlessly cruel. And this filters into the child's consciousness through his parents' tone of voice as he is being exhorted, punished, or loved; in the sudden, uncontrollable note of fear heard in his mother's or his father's voice when he has strayed beyond some particular boundary. He does not know what the boundary is, and he can get no explanation of it, which is frightening enough, but the fear he hears in the voices of his elders is more frightening still. The fear that I heard in my father's voice, for example, when he realized that I really *believed* I could do anything a white boy could do, and had every intention of proving it, was not at all like the fear I heard when one of us was ill or had fallen down the stairs or strayed too far from the house. It was another fear, a fear that the child, in challenging the white world's assumptions, was putting himself in the path of destruction. A child cannot, thank Heaven, know how vast and how merciless is the nature of power, with what unbelievable cruelty people treat each other. He reacts to the fear in his parents' voices because his parents hold up the world for him and he has no protection without them. I defended myself, as I imagined, against the fear my father made me feel by remembering that he was very old-fashioned. Also, I prided myself on the fact that I already knew how to outwit him. To defend oneself against a fear is simply to insure that one will, one day, be conquered by it; fears must be faced. As for one's wits, it is just not true that one can live by them—not, that is, if one wishes really to live. That summer, in any case, all the fears with which I had grown up, and which were now a part of me and controlled my vision of the world, rose up like a wall between the world and me, and drove me into the church.

As I look back, everything I did seems curiously deliberate, though it certainly did not seem deliberate then. For example, I did not join the church of which my father was a member and in which he preached. My best friend in school, who attended a different church, had already "surrendered his life to the Lord," and he was very anxious about my soul's salvation. (I wasn't, but any human attention was better than none.) One Saturday afternoon, he took me to his church. There were no services that day, and the church was empty, except for some women cleaning and some other women praying. My friend took me into the back room to meet his pastor—a woman. There she sat, in her robes, smiling, an extremely proud and handsome woman, with Africa, Europe, and the America of the American Indian blended in her face. She was perhaps forty-five or fifty at this time, and in our world she was a very celebrated woman. My friend was about to introduce me when she looked at me and smiled and said, "Whose little boy are you?" Now this, unbelievably, was precisely the phrase used by pimps and racketeers on the Avenue when they suggested, both humorously and intensely, that I "hang out" with them. Perhaps part of the terror they had caused me to feel came from the fact that I unquestionably wanted to be *somebody's* little boy. I was so frightened, and at the mercy of so many conundrums, that inevitably, that summer, *someone* would have taken me over; one doesn't, in Harlem, long remain standing on any auction block.

It was my good luck—perhaps—that I found myself in the church racket instead of some other, and surrendered to a spiritual seduction long before I came to any carnal knowledge. For when the pastor asked me, with that marvellous smile, "Whose little boy are you?" my heart replied at once, "Why, yours."

The summer wore on, and things got worse. I became more guilty and more frightened, and kept all this bottled up inside me, and naturally, inescapably, one night, when this woman had finished preaching, everything came roaring, screaming, crying out, and I fell to the ground before the altar. It was the strangest sensation I have ever had in my life—up to that time, or since. I had not known that it was going to happen, or that it could happen. One moment I was on my feet, singing and clapping and, at the same time, working out in my head the plot of a play I was working on then; the next moment, with no transition, no sensation of falling, I was on my back, with the lights beating down into my face and all the vertical saints above me. I did not know what I was doing down so low, or how I had got there. And the anguish that filled me cannot be described. It moved in me like one of those floods that devastate counties, tearing everything down, tearing children from their parents and lovers from each other, and making everything an unrecognizable waste. All I really remember is the pain, the unspeakable pain; it was as though I were yelling up to Heaven and Heaven would not hear me. And if Heaven would not hear me, if love could not descend from Heaven—to wash me, to make me clean—then utter disaster was my portion. Yes, it does indeed mean something—something unspeakable—to be born, in a white country, an Anglo-Teutonic, antisexual country, black. You very soon, without knowing it, give up all hope of communion. Black people, mainly, look down or look up but do not look at each other, not at you, and white people, mainly, look away. And the universe is simply a sounding drum; there is no way, no way whatever, so it seemed then and has sometimes seemed since, to get through a life, to love your wife and children, or your friends, or your mother and father, or to be loved. The universe, which is not merely the stars and the moon and the planets, flowers, grass, and trees, but *other people,* has evolved no terms for your existence, has made no room for you, and if love will not swing wide the gates, no other power will or can. And if one despairs—as who has not?—of human love, God's love alone is left. But God—and I felt this even then, so long ago, on that tremendous floor, unwillingly—

is white. And if His love was so great, and if He loved all His children, why were we, the blacks, cast down so far? Why? In spite of all I said thereafter, I found no answer on the floor—not *that* answer, anyway—and I was on the floor all night. Over me, to bring me "through," the saints sang and rejoiced and prayed. And in the morning, when they raised me, they told me that I was "saved."

Well, indeed I was, in a way, for I was utterly drained and exhausted, and released, for the first time, from all my guilty torment. I was aware then only of my relief. For many years, I could not ask myself why human relief had to be achieved in a fashion at once so pagan and so desperate—in a fashion at once so unspeakably old and so unutterably new. And by the time I was able to ask myself this question, I was also able to see that the principles governing the rites and customs of the churches in which I grew up did not differ from the principles governing the rites and customs of other churches, white. The principles were Blindness, Loneliness, and Terror, the first principle necessarily and actively cultivated in order to deny the two others. I would love to believe that the principles were Faith, Hope, and Charity, but this is clearly not so for most Christians, or for what we call the Christian world.

31

I was saved. But at the same time, out of a deep, adolescent cunning I do not pretend to understand, I realized immediately that I could not remain in the church merely as another worshipper. I would have to give myself something to do, in order not to be too bored and find myself among all the wretched unsaved of the Avenue. And I don't doubt that I also intended to best my father on his own ground. Anyway, very shortly after I joined the church, I became a preacher—a Young Minister— and I remained in the pulpit for more than three years. My youth quickly made me a much bigger drawing card than my father. I pushed this advantage ruthlessly, for it was the most effective means I had found of breaking his hold over me. That was the most frightening time of my life, and quite the most dishonest, and the resulting hysteria lent great passion to my sermons—for a while. I relished the attention and the relative immunity from punishment that my new status gave me, and I relished, above all, the sudden right to privacy. It had to be recognized, after all, that I was still a schoolboy, with my schoolwork to do, and I was also expected to prepare at least one sermon a week. During what we may call my heyday, I preached much more often than that. This meant that there were hours and even whole days when I could not be interrupted—not even by my father. I had im-mobilized him. It took rather more time for me to realize that I had also immobilized myself, and had escaped from nothing whatever.

The church was very exciting. It took a long time for me to disengage myself from this excitement, and on the blindest, most visceral level, I never really have, and never will. There is no music like that music, no drama like the drama of the saints rejoicing, the sinners moaning, the tambou-rines racing, and all those voices coming together and crying holy unto the Lord. There is still, for me, no pathos quite like the pathos of those multi-colored, worn, somehow triumphant and trans-figured faces, speaking from the depths of a visible, tangible, continuing despair of the goodness of the Lord. I have never seen anything to equal the fire and excitement that sometimes, without warning, fill a church, causing the church, as Leadbelly and so many others have testified, to "rock." Nothing that has happened to me since equals the power and the glory that I sometimes felt when, in the middle of a sermon, I knew that I was somehow, by some miracle, really carrying, as they said, "the Word"—when the church and I were one. Their pain and their joy were mine, and mine were theirs —they surrendered their pain and joy to me, I sur-

rendered mine to them—and their cries of "Amen!"
and "Hallelujah!" and "Yes, Lord!" and "Praise
His name!' and "Preach it, brother!" sustained and
whipped on my solos until we all became equal,
wringing wet, singing and dancing, in anguish and
rejoicing, at the foot of the altar. It was, for a long
time, in spite of—or, not inconceivably, because of—
the shabbiness of my motives, my only sustenance,
my meat and drink. I rushed home from school, to
the church, to the altar, to be alone there, to com-
mune with Jesus, my dearest Friend, who would
never fail me, who knew all the secrets of my
heart. Perhaps He did, but I didn't, and the bargain
we struck, actually, down there at the foot of the
cross, was that He would never let me find out.

He failed His bargain. He was a much better
Man than I took Him for. It happened, as things
do, imperceptibly, in many ways at once. I date it—
the slow crumbling of my faith, the pulverization
of my fortress—from the time, about a year after
I had begun to preach, when I began to read again.
I justified this desire by the fact that I was still in
school, and I began, fatally, with Dostoevski. By
this time, I was in a high school that was pre-
dominantly Jewish. This meant that I was surrounded by people who were, by definition, beyond
any hope of salvation, who laughed at the tracts

and leaflets I brought to school, and who pointed out that the Gospels had been written long after the death of Christ. This might not have been so distressing if it had not forced me to read the tracts and leaflets myself, for they were indeed, unless one believed their message already, impossible to believe. I remember feeling dimly that there was a kind of blackmail in it. People, I felt, ought to love the Lord *because* they loved Him, and not because they were afraid of going to Hell. I was forced, reluctantly, to realize that the Bible itself had been written by men, and translated by men out of languages I could not read, and I was already, without quite admitting it to myself, terribly involved with the effort of putting words on paper. Of course, I had the rebuttal ready: These men had all been operating under divine inspiration. *Had* they? *All* of them? And I also knew by now, alas, far more about divine inspiration than I dared admit, for I knew how I worked myself up into my own visions, and how frequently—indeed, incessantly—the visions God granted to me differed from the visions He granted to my father. I did not understand the dreams I had at night, but I knew that they were not holy. For that matter, I knew that my waking hours were far from holy. I spent most of my time in a state of repentance for things

I had vividly desired to do but had not done. The fact that I was dealing with Jews brought the whole question of color, which I had been desperately avoiding, into the terrified center of my mind. I realized that the Bible had been written by white men. I knew that, according to many Christians, I was a descendant of Ham, who had been cursed, and that I was therefore predestined to be a slave. This had nothing to do with anything I was, or contained, or could become; my fate had been sealed forever, from the beginning of time. And it seemed, indeed, when one looked out over Christendom, that this was what Christendom effectively believed. It was certainly the way it behaved. I remembered the Italian priests and bishops blessing Italian boys who were on their way to Ethiopia.

Again, the Jewish boys in high school were troubling because I could find no point of connection between them and the Jewish pawnbrokers and landlords and grocery-store owners in Harlem. I knew that these people were Jews—God knows I was told it often enough—but I thought of them only as white. Jews, as such, until I got to high school, were all incarcerated in the Old Testament, and their names were Abraham, Moses, Daniel, Ezekiel, and Job, and Shadrach, Meshach, and Abednego. It was bewildering to find them so many miles and centuries out of Egypt, and so far from the fiery furnace. My best friend in high school was a Jew. He came to our house once, and afterward my father asked, as he asked about everyone, "Is he a Christian?"—by which he meant "Is he saved?" I really do not know whether my answer came out of innocence or venom, but I said coldly, "No. He's Jewish." My father slammed me across the face with his great palm, and in that moment everything flooded back—all the hatred and all the fear, and the depth of a merciless resolve to kill my father rather than allow my father to kill me—and I knew that all those sermons and tears and all that repentance and rejoicing had changed nothing. I wondered if I was expected to be glad that a friend of mine, or anyone, was to be tormented forever in Hell, and I also thought, suddenly, of the Jews in another Christian nation, Germany. They were not so far from the fiery furnace after all, and my best friend might have been one of them. I told my father, "He's a better Christian than you are," and walked out of the house. The battle between us was in the open, but that was all right; it was almost a relief. A more deadly struggle had begun.

Being in the pulpit was like being in the theatre; I was behind the scenes and knew how the illusion was worked. I knew the other ministers and knew the quality of their lives. And I don't mean to suggest by this the "Elmer Gantry" sort of hypocrisy concerning sensuality; it was a deeper, deadlier, and more subtle hypocrisy than that, and a little honest sensuality, or a lot, would have been like water in an extremely bitter desert. I knew how to work on a congregation until the last dime was surrendered —it was not very hard to do—and I knew where the money for "the Lord's work" went. I knew, though I did not wish to know it, that I had no respect for the people with whom I worked. I could not have said it then, but I also knew that if I continued I would soon have no respect for myself. And the fact that I was "the young Brother Baldwin" increased my value with those same pimps and racketeers who had helped to stampede me into the church in the first place. They still saw the little boy they intended to take over. They were waiting for me to come to my senses and realize that I was in a very lucrative business. They knew that I did not yet realize this, and also that I had not yet begun to suspect where my own needs, *coming up* (they were very patient), could drive me. They themselves did know the score, and they knew that the odds were in their favor, And, really, I knew it, too. I was even lonelier and more vulnerable than I had been before. And the blood of the Lamb had not cleansed me in any way whatever. I was just as black as I had been the day that I was born. Therefore, when I faced a congregation, it began to take all the strength I had not to stammer, not to curse, not to tell them to throw away their Bibles and get off their knees and go home and organize, for example, a rent strike. When I watched all the children, their copper, brown, and beige faces staring up at me as I taught Sunday school, I felt that I was committing a crime in talking about the gentle Jesus, in telling them to reconcile themselves to their misery on earth in order to gain the crown of eternal life. Were only Negroes to gain this crown? Was Heaven, then, to be merely another ghetto? Perhaps I might have been able to reconcile myself even to this if I had been able to believe that there was any loving-kindness to be found in the haven I represented. But I had been in the pulpit too long and I had seen too many monstrous things. I don't refer merely to the glaring fact that the minister eventually acquires houses and Cadillacs while the faithful continue to scrub floors and drop their dimes and quarters and dollars into the plate. I really mean that there was no love in the church. It was a mask for hatred and self-hatred and despair. The transfiguring power of the Holy Ghost ended when the service ended, and salvation stopped at

the church door. When we were told to love everybody, I had thought that that meant *everybody*.
But no. It applied only to those who believed as we
did, and it did not apply to white people at all.
I was told by a minister, for example, that I should
never, on any public conveyance, under any circumstances, rise and give my seat to a white woman.
White men never rose for Negro women. Well,
that was true enough, in the main—I saw his point.
But what was the point, the purpose, of *my* salvation if it did not permit me to behave with love
toward others, no matter how they behaved toward
me? What others did was their responsibility, for
which they would answer when the judgment
trumpet sounded. But what *I* did was *my* responsibility, and I would have to answer, too—unless, of
course, there was also in Heaven a special dispensa-
tion for the benighted black, who was not to be
judged in the same way as other human beings, or
angels. It probably occurred to me around this time
that the vision people hold of the world to come
is but a reflection, with predictable wishful dis-
tortions, of the world in which they live. And this
did not apply only to Negroes, who were no more
"simple" or "spontaneous" or "Christian" than
anybody else—who were merely more oppressed.
In the same way that we, for white people, were

the descendants of Ham, and were cursed forever, white people were, for us, the descendants of Cain. And the passion with which we loved the Lord was a measure of how deeply we feared and distrusted and, in the end, hated almost all strangers, always, and avoided and despised ourselves.

But I cannot leave it at that; there is more to it than that. In spite of everything, there was in the life I fled a zest and a joy and a capacity for facing and surviving disaster that are very moving and very rare. Perhaps we were, all of us—pimps, whores, racketeers, church members, and children —bound together by the nature of our oppression, the specific and peculiar complex of risks we had to run; if so, within these limits we sometimes achieved with each other a freedom that was close to love. I remember, anyway, church suppers and outings, and, later, after I left the church, rent and waistline parties where rage and sorrow sat in the darkness and did not stir, and we ate and drank and talked and laughed and danced and forgot all about "the man." We had the liquor, the chicken, the music, and each other, and had no need to pretend to be what we were not. This is the freedom that one hears in some gospel songs, for example, and in jazz. In all jazz, and especially in the blues, there is something tart and ironic, authoritative and double-edged. White Americans seem to feel that happy songs are *happy* and sad songs are *sad,* and that, God help us, is exactly the way most white Americans sing them—sounding, in both cases, so helplessly, defenselessly fatuous that one dare not speculate on the temperature of the deep freeze from which issue their brave and sexless little voices. Only people who have been "down the line," as the song puts it, know what this music is about. I think it was Big Bill Broonzy who used to sing "I Feel So Good," a really joyful song about a man who is on his way to the railroad station to meet his girl. She's coming home. It is the singer's incredibly moving exuberance that makes one realize how leaden the time must have been while she was gone. There is no guarantee that she will stay this time, either, as the singer clearly knows, and, in fact, she has not yet actually arrived. Tonight, or tomorrow, or within the next five minutes, he may very well be singing "Lonesome in My Bedroom," or insisting, "Ain't we, ain't we, going to make it all right? Well, if we don't today, we will tomorrow night." White Americans do not understand the depths out of which such an ironic tenacity comes, but they suspect that the force is sensual, and they are terrified of sensuality and do not any longer understand it. The word "sensual" is not intended to bring to mind quivering dusky maidens or priapic black studs. I am referring to something much simpler and much less fanciful. To be sensual, I think, is to respect and rejoice in the force of life, of life itself, and to be *present* in all that one does, from the effort of loving to the breaking of bread. It will be a great day for America, incidentally, when we begin to eat bread again, instead of the blasphemous and tasteless foam rubber that we have substituted for it. And I am not being frivolous now, either. Something very sinister happens to the people of a country when they begin to distrust their own reactions as deeply as they do here, and become as joyless as they have become. It is this individual uncertainty on the part of white American men and women, this inability to renew themselves at the fountain of their own lives, that makes the discussion, let alone elucidation, of any conundrum—that is, any reality—so supremely difficult. The person who distrusts himself has no touchstone for reality—for this touchstone can be only oneself. Such a person interposes between himself and reality nothing less than a labyrinth of attitudes. And these attitudes, furthermore, though the person is usually unaware of it (is unaware of so much!), are historical and public attitudes. They do not relate to the present any more than they relate to the person. Therefore, whatever white people do not know about Negroes reveals, precisely and inexorably, what they do not know about themselves.

White Christians have also forgotten several elementary historical details. They have forgotten that the religion that is now identified with their virtue and their power—"God is on our side," says Dr. Verwoerd—came out of a rocky piece of ground in what is now known as the Middle East before color was invented, and that in order for the Christian church to be established, Christ had to be put to death, by Rome, and that the real architect of the Christian church was not the disreputable, sun-baked Hebrew who gave it his name but the mercilessly fanatical and self-righteous St. Paul. The energy that was buried with the rise of the Christian nations must come back into the world; nothing can prevent it. Many of us, I think, both long to see this happen and are terrified of it, for though this transformation contains the hope of liberation, it also imposes a necessity for great change. But in order to deal with the untapped and dormant force of the previously subjugated, in order to survive as a human, moving, moral weight in the world, America and all the Western nations will be forced to reëxamine themselves and release themselves

44

from many things that are now taken to be sacred, and to discard nearly all the assumptions that have been used to justify their lives and their anguish and their crimes so long.

"The white man's Heaven," sings a Black Muslim minister, "is the black man's Hell." One may object —possibly—that this puts the matter somewhat too simply, but the song is true, and it has been true for as long as white men have ruled the world. The Africans put it another way: When the white man came to Africa, the white man had the Bible and the African had the land, but now it is the white man who is being, reluctantly and bloodily, separated from the land, and the African who is still attempting to digest or to vomit up the Bible. The struggle, therefore, that now begins in the world is extremely complex, involving the historical role of Christianity in the realm of power—that is, politics— and in the realm of morals. In the realm of power, Christianity has operated with an unmitigated arrogance and cruelty—necessarily, since a religion ordinarily imposes on those who have discovered the true faith the spiritual duty of liberating the infidels. This particular true faith, moreover, is more deeply concerned about the soul than it is about the body, to which fact the flesh (and the corpses) of countless infidels bears witness. It goes without saying, then, that whoever questions the authority of the true faith also contests the right of the nations that hold this faith to rule over him—contests, in short, their title to his land. The spreading of the Gospel, regardless of the motives or the integrity or the heroism of some of the missionaries, was an absolutely indispensable justification for the planting of the flag. Priests and nuns and school-teachers helped to protect and sanctify the power that was so ruthlessly being used by people who were indeed seeking a city, but not one in the heavens, and one to be made, very definitely, by captive hands. The Christian church itself—again, as distinguished from some of its ministers—sanctified and rejoiced in the conquests of the flag, and encouraged, if it did not formulate, the belief that conquest, with the resulting relative well-being of the Western populations, was proof of the favor of God. God had come a long way from the desert—but then so had Allah, though in a very different direction. God, going north, and rising on the wings of power, had become white, and Allah, out of power, and on the dark side of Heaven, had become—for all practical purposes, anyway—black. Thus, in the realm of morals the role of Christianity has been, at best, ambivalent. Even leaving out of account the remarkable arrogance that assumed that the ways and morals of others were inferior to those of Christians, and that they therefore had every right, and could use any means, to change them, the collision between cultures—and the schizophrenia in the mind of Christendom—had rendered the domain of morals as chartless as the sea once was, and as treacherous as the sea still is. It is not too much to say that whoever wishes to become a truly moral human being (and let us not ask whether or not this is possible; I think we must *believe* that it is possible) must first divorce himself from all the prohibitions, crimes, and hypocrisies of the Christian church. If the concept of God has any validity or any use, it can only be to make us larger, freer, and more loving. If God cannot do this, then it is time we got rid of Him.

I HAD HEARD a great deal, long before I finally met him, of the Honorable Elijah Muhammad, and of the Nation of Islam movement, of which he is the leader. I paid very little attention to what I heard, because the burden of his message did not strike me as being very original; I had been hearing variations of it all my life. I sometimes found myself in Harlem on Saturday nights, and I stood in the crowds, at 125th Street and Seventh Avenue, and listened to the Muslim speakers. But I had heard

47

hundreds of such speeches—or so it seemed to me
at first. Anyway, I have long had a very definite
tendency to tune out the moment I come anywhere
near either a pulpit or a soapbox. What these men
were saying about white people I had often heard
before. And I dismissed the Nation of Islam's demand for a separate black economy in America,
which I had also heard before, as willful, and even
mischievous, nonsense. Then two things caused me
to begin to listen to the speeches, and one was the
behavior of the police. After all, I had seen men
dragged from their platforms on this very corner
for saying less virulent things, and I had seen many
crowds dispersed by policemen, with clubs or on
horseback. But the policemen were doing nothing
now. Obviously, this was not because they had become more human but because they were under
orders and because they were afraid. And indeed
they were, and I was delighted to see it. There they
stood, in twos and threes and fours, in their Cub
Scout uniforms and with their Cub Scout faces,
totally unprepared, as is the way with American he-
men, for anything that could not be settled with a
club or a fist or a gun. I might have pitied them if
I had not found myself in their hands so often and
discovered, through ugly experience, what they
were like when *they* held the power and what they

were like when *you* held the power. The behavior of the crowd, its silent intensity, was the other thing that forced me to reassess the speakers and their message. I sometimes think, with despair, that Americans will swallow whole any political speech whatever—we've been doing very little else, these last, bad years—so it may not mean anything to say that this sense of integrity, after what Harlem, especially, has been through in the way of demagogues, was a very startling change. Still, the speakers had an air of utter dedication, and the people looked toward them with a kind of intelligence of hope on their faces—not as though they were being consoled or drugged but as though they were being jolted.

Power was the subject of the speeches I heard. We were offered, as Nation of Islam doctrine, historical and divine proof that all white people are cursed, and are devils, and are about to be brought down. This has been revealed by Allah Himself to His prophet, the Honorable Elijah Muhammad. The white man's rule will be ended forever in ten or fifteen years (and it must be conceded that all present signs would seem to bear witness to the accuracy of the prophet's statement). The crowd seemed to swallow this theology with no effort—all crowds do swallow theology this way, I gather, in both sides of Jerusalem, in Istanbul, and in Rome—and, as

49

theology goes, it was no more indigestible than the more familiar brand asserting that there is a curse on the sons of Ham. No more, and no less, and it had been designed for the same purpose; namely, the sanctification of power. But very little time was spent on theology, for one did not need to prove to a Harlem audience that all white men were devils. They were merely glad to have, at last, divine corroboration of their experience, to hear—and it was a tremendous thing to hear—that they had been lied to for all these years and generations, and that their captivity was ending, for God was black. Why were they *hearing* it now, since this was not the first time it had been said? I had heard it many times, from various prophets, during all the years that I was growing up. Elijah Muhammad himself has now been carrying the same message for more than thirty years; he is not an overnight sensation, and we owe his ministry, I am told, to the fact that when he was a child of six or so, his father was lynched before his eyes. (So much for states' rights.) And now, suddenly, people who have never before been able to hear this message hear it, and believe it, and are changed. Elijah Muhammad has been able to do what generations of welfare workers and committees and resolutions and reports and housing projects and playgrounds have failed to do: to heal

and redeem drunkards and junkies, to convert people who have come out of prison and to keep them
out, to make men chaste and women virtuous, and
to invest both the male and the female with a pride
and a serenity that hang about them like an unfail-
ing light. He has done all these things, which our
Christian church has spectacularly failed to do.
How has Elijah managed it?

Well, in a way—and I have no wish to minimize
his peculiar role and his peculiar achievement—it
is not he who has done it but time. Time catches up
with kingdoms and crushes them, gets its teeth into
doctrines and rends them; time reveals the foundations on which any kingdom rests, and eats at those
foundations, and it destroys doctrines by proving
them to be untrue. In those days, not so very long
ago, when the priests of that church which stands
in Rome gave God's blessing to Italian boys being
sent out to ravage a defenseless black country—
which until that event, incidentally, had not considered itself to be black—it was not possible to believe in a black God. To entertain such a belief
would have been to entertain madness. But time has
passed, and in that time the Christian world has revealed itself as morally bankrupt and politically un-
stable. The Tunisians were quite right in 1956—and
it was a very significant moment in Western (and

African) history—when they countered the French justification for remaining in North Africa with the question "Are the *French* ready for self-government?" Again, the terms "civilized" and "Christian" begin to have a very strange ring, particularly in the ears of those who have been judged to be neither civilized nor Christian, when a Christian nation surrenders to a foul and violent orgy, as Germany did during the Third Reich. For the crime of their ancestry, millions of people in the middle of the twentieth century, and in the heart of Europe —God's citadel—were sent to a death so calculated, so hideous, and so prolonged that no age before this enlightened one had been able to imagine it, much less achieve and record it. Furthermore, those beneath the Western heel, unlike those within the West, are aware that Germany's current role in Europe is to act as a bulwark against the "uncivilized" hordes, and since power is what the powerless want, they understand very well what we of the West want to keep, and are not deluded by our talk of a freedom that we have never been willing to share with them. From my own point of view, the fact of the Third Reich alone makes obsolete forever any question of Christian superiority, except in technological terms. White people were, and are, astounded by the holocaust in Germany.

They did not know that they could act that way. But I very much doubt whether black people were astounded—at least, in the same way. For my part, the fate of the Jews, and the world's indifference to it, frightened me very much. I could not but feel, in those sorrowful years, that this human indifference, concerning which I knew so much already, would be my portion on the day that the United States decided to murder its Negroes systematically instead of little by little and catch-as-catch-can. I was, of course, authoritatively assured that what had happened to the Jews in Germany could not happen to the Negroes in America, but I thought, bleakly, that the German Jews had probably believed similar counsellors, and, again, I could not share the white man's vision of himself for the very good reason that white men in America do not behave toward black men the way they behave toward each other. When a white man faces a black man, especially if the black man is helpless, terrible things are revealed. I know. I have been carried into precinct basements often enough, and I have seen and heard and endured the secrets of desperate white men and women, which they knew were safe with me, because even if I should speak, no one would believe me. And they would not believe me precisely because they would know that what I said was true.

The treatment accorded the Negro during the Second World War marks, for me, a turning point in the Negro's relation to America. To put it briefly, and somewhat too simply, a certain hope died, a certain respect for white Americans faded. One began to pity them, or to hate them. You must put yourself in the skin of a man who is wearing the uniform of his country, is a candidate for death in its defense, and who is called a "nigger" by his comrades-in-arms and his officers; who is almost always given the hardest, ugliest, most menial work to do; who knows that the white G.I. has informed the Europeans that he is subhuman (so much for the American male's sexual security); who does not dance at the U.S.O. the night white soldiers dance there, and does not drink in the same bars white soldiers drink in; and who watches German prisoners of war being treated by Americans with more human dignity than he has ever received at their hands. And who, at the same time, as a human being, is far freer in a strange land than he has ever been at home. *Home!* The very word begins to have a despairing and diabolical ring. You must consider what happens to this citizen, after all he has endured, when he returns—home: search, in his shoes, for a job, for a place to live; ride, in his skin, on segregated buses; see, with his eyes, the signs saying "White" and "Colored," and especially the signs that say "White Ladies" and "Colored *Women*"; look into the eyes of his wife; look into the eyes of his son; listen, with his ears, to political speeches, North and South; imagine yourself being told to "wait." And all this is happening in the richest and freest country in the world, and in the middle of the twentieth century. The subtle and deadly change of heart that might occur in you would be involved with the realization that a civilization is not destroyed by wicked people; it is not necessary that people be wicked but only that they be spineless. I and two Negro acquaintances, all of us well past thirty, and looking it, were in the bar of Chicago's O'Hare Airport several months ago, and the bartender refused to serve us, because, he said, we looked too young. It took a vast amount of patience not to strangle him, and great insistence and some luck to get the manager, who defended his bartender on the ground that he was "new" and had not yet, presumably, learned how to distinguish between a Negro boy of twenty and a Negro "boy" of thirty-seven. Well, we were served, finally, of course, but by this time no amount of Scotch would have helped us. The bar was very crowded, and our altercation had been extremely noisy; not one customer in the bar had done anything to help us. When it was over, and the three of us stood at the bar trembling with rage and frustration, and drinking—and trapped, now, in the airport, for we had deliberately come early in order to have a few drinks and to eat—a young white man standing near us asked if we were students. I suppose he thought that this was the only possible explanation for our putting up a fight. I told him that he hadn't wanted to talk to us earlier and we didn't want to talk to him now. The reply visibly hurt his feelings, and this, in turn, caused me to despise him. But when one of us, a Korean War veteran, told this young man that the fight we had been having in the bar had been his fight, too, the young man said, "I lost my conscience a long time ago," and turned and walked out. I know that one would rather not think so, but this young man is typical. So, on the basis of the evidence, had everyone else in the bar lost *his* conscience. A few years ago, I would have hated these people with all my heart. Now I pitied them, pitied them in order not to despise them. And this is not the happiest way to feel toward one's countrymen.

But, in the end, it is the threat of universal extinction hanging over all the world today that changes, totally and forever, the nature of reality and brings into devastating question the true meaning of man's history. We human beings now have the power to exterminate ourselves; this seems to be the entire sum of our achievement. We have taken this journey and arrived at this place in God's name. This, then, is the best that God (the white God) can do. If that is so, then it is time to replace Him—replace Him with what? And this void, this despair, this torment is felt everywhere in the West, from the streets of Stockholm to the churches of New Orleans and the sidewalks of Harlem.

God is black. All black men belong to Islam; they have been chosen. And Islam shall rule the world. The dream, the sentiment is old; only the color is new. And it is this dream, this sweet possibility, that thousands of oppressed black men and women in this country now carry away with them after the Muslim minister has spoken, through the dark, noisome ghetto streets, into the hovels where so many have perished. The white God has not delivered them; perhaps the Black God will.

While I was in Chicago last summer, the Honorable Elijah Muhammad invited me to have dinner at his home. This is a stately mansion on Chicago's South Side, and it is the headquarters of the Nation of Islam movement. I had not gone to Chicago to meet Elijah Muhammad—he was not in my thoughts at all—but the moment I received the invitation, it occurred to me that I ought to have expected it. In a way, I owe the invitation to the incredible, abysmal, and really cowardly obtuseness of white liberals. Whether in private debate or in public, any attempt I made to explain how the Black Muslim movement came about, and how it has achieved such force, was met with a blankness that revealed the little connection that the liberals' attitudes have with their perceptions or their lives, or even their knowledge—revealed, in fact, that they could deal with the Negro as a symbol or a victim but had no sense of him as a man. When Malcolm X, who is considered the movement's second-in-command, and heir apparent, points out that the cry of "violence" was not raised, for example, when the Israelis fought to regain Israel, and, indeed, is raised only when black men indicate that they will fight for *their* rights, he is speaking the truth. The conquests of England, every single one of them bloody, are part of what Americans have in mind when they speak of England's glory. In the United States, violence and heroism have been made synonymous except when it comes to blacks, and the only way to defeat Malcolm's point is to concede it and then ask oneself why this is so. Malcolm's statement is *not*

answered by references to the triumphs of the
N.A.A.C.P., the more particularly since very few
liberals have any notion of how long, how costly,
and how heartbreaking a task it is to gather the
evidence that one can carry into court, or how long
such court battles take. Neither is it answered by
references to the student sit-in-movement, if only
because not all Negroes are students and not all of
them live in the South. I, in any case, certainly refuse to be put in the position of denying the truth of
Malcolm's statements simply because I disagree with
his conclusions, or in order to pacify the liberal
conscience. Things are as bad as the Muslims say
they are—in fact, they are worse, and the Muslims
do not help matters—but there *is* no reason that
black men should be expected to be more patient,
more forbearing, more farseeing than whites; indeed, quite the contrary. The real reason that non-
violence is considered to be a virtue in Negroes—
I am not speaking now of its racial value, another
matter altogether—is that white men do not want
their lives, their self-image, or their property threatened. One wishes they would say so more often.
At the end of a television program on which Malcolm X and I both appeared, Malcolm was stopped
by a white member of the audience who said, "I
have a thousand dollars and an acre of land. What's

59

going to happen to me?" I admired the directness of the man's question, but I didn't hear Malcolm's reply, because I was trying to explain to someone else that the situation of the Irish a hundred years ago and the situation of the Negro today cannot very usefully be compared. Negroes were brought here in chains long before the Irish ever thought of leaving Ireland; what manner of consolation is it to be told that emigrants arriving here—voluntarily—long after you did have risen far above you? In the hall, as I was waiting for the elevator, someone shook my hand and said, "Goodbye, Mr. James Baldwin. We'll soon be addressing you as Mr. James X." And I thought, for an awful moment, My God, if this goes on much longer, you probably will. Elijah Muhammad had seen this show, I think, or another one, and he had been told about me. Therefore, late on a hot Sunday afternoon, I presented myself at his door.

I was frightened, because I had, in effect, been summoned into a royal presence. I was frightened for another reason, too. I knew the tension in me between love and power, between pain and rage, and the curious, the grinding way I remained extended between these poles—perpetually attempting to choose the better rather than the worse. But this choice was a choice in terms of a personal, a private better (I was, after all, a writer); what was its relevance in terms of a social worse? Here was the South Side—a million in captivity—stretching from this doorstep as far as the eye could see. And they didn't even read; depressed populations don't have the time or energy to spare. The affluent populations, which should have been their help, didn't, as far as could be discovered, read, either—they merely bought books and devoured them, but not in order to learn: in order to learn new attitudes. Also, I knew that once I had entered the house, I couldn't smoke or drink, and I felt guilty about the cigarettes in my pocket, as I had felt years ago when my friend first took me into his church. I was half an hour late, having got lost on the way here, and I felt as deserving of a scolding as a schoolboy.

The young man who came to the door—he was about thirty, perhaps, with a handsome, smiling face—didn't seem to find my lateness offensive, and led me into a large room. On one side of the room sat half a dozen women, all in white; they were much occupied with a beautiful baby, who seemed to belong to the youngest of the women. On the other side of the room sat seven or eight men, young, dressed in dark suits, very much at ease, and very imposing. The sunlight came into the room with the peacefulness one remembers from rooms in one's

61

early childhood—a sunlight encountered later only in one's dreams. I remember being astounded by the quietness, the ease, the peace, the taste. I was introduced, they greeted me with a genuine cordiality and respect—and the respect increased my fright, for it meant that they expected something of me that I knew in my heart, for their sakes, I could not give—and we sat down. Elijah Muhammad was not in the room. Conversation was slow, but not as stiff as I had feared it would be. They kept it going, for I simply did not know which subjects I could acceptably bring up. They knew more about me, and had read more of what I had written, than I had expected, and I wondered what they made of it all, what they took my usefulness to be. The women were carrying on their own conversation, in low tones; I gathered that they were not expected to take part in male conversations. A few women kept coming in and out of the room, apparently making preparations for dinner. We, the men, did not plunge deeply into any subject, for, clearly, we were all waiting for the appearance of Elijah. Presently, the men, one by one, left the room and returned. Then I was asked if I would like to wash, and I, too, walked down the hall to the bathroom. Shortly after I came back, we stood up, and Elijah entered.

I do not know what I had expected to see. I had read some of his speeches, and had heard fragments of others on the radio and on television, so I associated him with ferocity. But, no—the man who came into the room was small and slender, really very delicately put together, with a thin face, large, warm eyes, and a most winning smile. Something came into the room with him—his disciples' joy at seeing him, his joy at seeing them. It was the kind of encounter one watches with a smile simply because it is so rare that people enjoy one another. He teased the women, like a father, with no hint of that ugly and unctuous flirtatiousness I knew so well from other churches, and they responded like that, with great freedom and yet from a great and loving distance. He had seen me when he came into the room, I knew, though he had not looked my way. I had the feeling, as he talked and laughed with the others, whom I could only think of as his children, that he was sizing me up, deciding something. Now he turned toward me, to welcome me, with that marvellous smile, and carried me back nearly twenty-four years, to that moment when the pastor had smiled at me and said, "Whose little boy are you?" I did not respond now as I had responded then, because there are some things (not many, alas!) that one cannot do twice. But I knew what he made me feel, how I was drawn toward his peculiar authority, how his smile promised to take the burden of my life off my shoulders. *Take your burdens to the Lord and leave them there.* The central quality in Elijah's face is pain, and his smile is a witness to it—pain so old and deep and black that it becomes personal and particular only when he smiles. One wonders what he would sound like if he could sing. He turned to me, with that smile, and said something like "I've got a lot to say to *you,* but we'll wait until we sit *down.*" And I laughed. He made me think of my father and me as we might have been if we had been friends.

In the dining room, there were two long tables; the men sat at one and the women at the other. Elijah was at the head of our table, and I was seated at his left. I can scarcely remember what we ate, except that it was plentiful, sane, and simple—so sane and simple that it made me feel extremely decadent, and I think that I drank, therefore, two glasses of milk. Elijah mentioned having seen me on television and said that it seemed to him that I was not yet brainwashed and was trying to become myself. He said this in a curiously unnerving way, his eyes looking into mine and one hand half hiding his lips, as though he were trying to conceal bad teeth. But his teeth were not bad. Then I remembered hearing that he had spent time in prison. I suppose that I *would* like to become myself, whatever that may mean, but I knew that Elijah's meaning and mine were not the same. I said yes, I was trying to be me, but I did not know how to say more than that, and so I waited.

Whenever Elijah spoke, a kind of chorus arose from the table, saying "Yes, that's right." This began to set my teeth on edge. And Elijah himself had a further, unnerving habit, which was to ricochet his questions and comments off someone else on their way to you. Now, turning to the man on his right, he began to speak of the white devils with whom I had last appeared on TV: What had they made *him* (me) feel? I could not answer this and was not absolutely certain that I was expected to. The people referred to had certainly made me feel exasperated and useless, but I did not think of them as devils. Elijah went on about the crimes of white people, to this endless chorus of "Yes, that's right." Someone at the table said. "The white man sure *is* a devil. He proves that by his own actions." I looked around. It was a very young man who had said this, scarcely more than a boy—very dark and sober, very bitter. Elijah began to speak of the Christian religion, of Christians, in the same soft, joking way.

I began to see that Elijah's power came from his single-mindedness. There is nothing calculated about him; he means every word he says. The real reason, according to Elijah, that I failed to realize that the white man was a devil was that I had been too long exposed to white teaching and had never received true instruction. "The so-called American Negro" is the only reason Allah has permitted the United States to endure so long; the white man's time was up in 1913, but it is the will of Allah that this lost black nation, the black men of this country, be redeemed from their white masters and returned to the true faith, which is Islam. Until this is done—and it will be accomplished very soon—the total destruction of the white man is being delayed. Elijah's mission is to return "the so-called Negro" to Islam, to separate the chosen of Allah from this doomed nation. Furthermore, the white man knows his history, knows himself to be a devil, and knows that his time is running out, and all his technology, psychology, science, and "tricknology" are being expended in the effort to prevent black men from hearing the truth. This truth is that at the very beginning of time there was not one white face to be found in all the universe. Black men ruled the earth and the black man was perfect. This is the truth concerning the era that white men now refer to as prehistoric. They want black men to believe that they, like white men, once lived in caves and swung from trees and ate their meat raw and did not have the power of speech. But this is not true. Black men were never in such a condition. Allah allowed the Devil, through his scientists, to carry on infernal experiments, which resulted, finally, in the creation of the devil known as the white man, and later, even more disastrously, in the creation of the white woman. And it was decreed that these monstrous creatures should rule the earth for a certain number of years—I forget how many thousand, but, in any case, their rule now is ending, and Allah, who had never approved of the creation of the white man in the first place (who knows him, in fact, to be not a man at all but a devil), is anxious to restore the rule of peace that the rise of the white man totally destroyed. There is thus, by definition, no virtue in white people, and since they are another creation entirely and can no more, by breeding, become black than a cat, by breeding, can become a horse, there is no hope for them.

There is nothing new in this merciless formulation except the explicitness of its symbols and the candor of its hatred. Its emotional tone is as familiar to me as my own skin; it is but another way of saying that *sinners shall be bound in Hell a thousand years.* That sinners have always, for American Negroes, been white is a truth we needn't labor, and every American Negro, therefore, risks having the gates of paranoia close on him. In a society that is entirely hostile, and, by its nature, seems determined to cut you down—that has cut down so many in the past and cuts down so many every day—it begins to be almost impossible to distinguish a real from a fancied injury. One can very quickly cease to attempt this distinction, and, what is worse, one usually ceases to attempt it without realizing that one has done so. All doormen, for example, and all policemen have by now, for me, become exactly the same, and my style with them is designed simply to intimidate them before they can intimidate me. No doubt I am guilty of some injustice here, but it is irreducible, since I cannot risk assuming that the humanity of these people is more real to them than their uniforms. Most Negroes cannot risk assuming that the humanity of white people is more real to them than their color. And this leads, imperceptibly but inevitably, to a state of mind in which, having long ago learned to expect the worst, one finds it very easy to believe the worst. The brutality with which Negroes are treated in this country simply cannot be overstated, however unwilling white men may be to hear it. In the beginning—and neither can this be overstated—a Negro just cannot *believe* that white people are treating him as they do; he does not know what he has done to merit it. And when he realizes that the treatment accorded him has nothing to do with anything he has done, that the attempt of white people to destroy him—for that is what it is—is utterly gratuitous, it is not hard for him to think of white people as devils. For the horrors of the American Negro's life there has been almost no language. The privacy of his experience, which is only beginning to be recognized in language, and which is denied or ignored in official and popular speech—hence the Negro idiom—lends credibility to any system that pretends to clarify it. And, in fact, the truth about the black man, as a historical entity and as a human being, *has* been hidden from him, deliberately and cruelly; the power of the white world is threatened whenever a black man refuses to accept the white world's definitions. So every attempt is made to cut that black man down—not only was made yesterday but is made today. Who, then, is to say with authority where the root of so much anguish and evil lies? Why, then, is it not possible that all things began with the black man and that he was perfect—especially since this is precisely the claim that white people have put forward for themselves all these years? Furthermore, it is now absolutely clear that white people are a minority in the world—so severe a minority that they now look rather more like an invention—and that they cannot possibly hope to rule it any longer. If this is so, why is it not also possible that they achieved their original dominance by stealth and cunning and bloodshed and in opposition to the will of Heaven, and not, as they claim, by Heaven's will? And if *this* is so, then the sword they have used so long against others can now, without mercy, be used against them. Heavenly witnesses are a tricky lot, to be used by whoever is closest to Heaven at the time. And legend and theology, which are designed to sanctify our fears, crimes, and aspirations, also reveal them for what they are.

I said, at last, in answer to some other ricocheted questions, "I left the church twenty years ago and I haven't joined anything since." It was my way of saying that I did not intend to join their movement, either.

"And what are you now?" Elijah asked.

I was in something of a bind, for I really could not say—could not allow myself to be stampeded into saying—that I was a Christian. "I? Now? Nothing." This was not enough. "I'm a writer. I like doing things alone." I heard myself saying this.

Elijah smiled at me. "I don't, anyway," I said, finally, "think about it a great deal."

Elijah said, to his right, "I think he ought to think about it *all* the deal," and with this the table agreed. But there was nothing malicious or condemnatory in it. I had the stifling feeling that *they* knew I belonged to them but knew that I did not know it yet, that I remained unready, and that they were simply waiting, patiently, and with assurance, for me to discover the truth for myself. For where else, after all, could I go? I was black, and therefore a part of Islam, and would be saved from the holocaust awaiting the white world whether I would or no. My weak, deluded scruples could avail nothing against the iron word of the prophet.

I felt that I was back in my father's house—as, indeed, in a way, I was—and I told Elijah that *I* did not care if white and black people married, and that I had many white friends. I would have no choice, if it came to it, but to perish with them, for (I said to myself, but not to Elijah), "I love a few people and they love me and some of them are white, and isn't love more important than color?"

Elijah looked at me with great kindness and affection, great pity, as though he were reading my heart, and indicated, skeptically, that I *might* have white friends, or think I did, and they *might* be trying to be decent—now—but their time was up. It was almost as though he were saying, "They had their chance, man, and they goofed!"

And I looked around the table. I certainly had no evidence to give them that would outweigh Elijah's authority or the evidence of their own lives or the reality of the streets outside. Yes, I knew two or three people, white, whom I would trust with my life, and I knew a few others, white, who were struggling as hard as they knew how, and with great effort and sweat and risk, to make the world more human. But how could I say this? One cannot argue with anyone's experience or decision or belief. All my evidence would be thrown out of court as ir-relevant to the main body of the case, for I could cite only exceptions. The South Side proved the justice of the indictment; the state of the world proved the justice of the indictment. Everything else, stretching back throughout recorded time, was merely a history of those exceptions who had tried to change the world and had failed. Was this true? *Had* they failed? How much depended on the point of view? For it would seem that a certain category of exceptions never failed to make the world worse —that category, precisely, for whom power is more real than love. And yet power *is* real, and many things, including, very often, love, cannot be achieved without it. In the eeriest way possible, I suddenly had a glimpse of what white people must go through at a dinner table when they are trying to prove that Negroes are not subhuman. I had almost said, after all, "Well, take my friend Mary," and very nearly descended to a catalogue of those virtues that gave Mary the right to be alive. And in what hope? That Elijah and the others would nod their heads solemnly and say, at least, "Well, *she's* all right—but the *others!"*

And I looked again at the young faces around the table, and looked back at Elijah, who was saying that no people in history had ever been respected who had not owned their land. And the table said, "Yes, that's right." I could not deny the truth of this statement. For everyone else has, *is*, a nation, with a specific location and a flag—even, these days, the Jew. It is only "the so-called American Negro" who remains trapped, disinherited, and despised, in a nation that has kept him in bondage for nearly four hundred years and is still unable to recognize him as a human being. And the Black Muslims, along with many people who are not Muslims, no longer wish for a recognition so grudging and (should it ever be achieved) so tardy. Again, it cannot be denied that this point of view is abundantly justified by American Negro history. It is galling indeed to have stood so long, hat in hand, waiting for Americans to grow up enough to realiz that you do not threaten them. On the other hand, how is the American Negro now to form himself into a separate nation? For this—and not only from the Muslim point of view—would seem to be his only hope of not perishing in the American backwater and being entirely and forever forgotten, as though he had never existed at all and his travail had been for nothing.

Elijah's intensity and the bitter isolation and disaffection of these young men and the despair of the streets outside had caused me to glimpse dimly what may now seem to be a fantasy, although, in an age so fantastical, I would hesitate to say precisely what a fantasy is. Let us say that the Muslims were to achieve the possession of the six or seven states that they claim are owed to Negroes by the United States as "back payment" for slave labor. Clearly, the United States would never surrender this territory, on any terms whatever, unless it found it impossible, for whatever reason, to hold it—unless, that is, the United States were to be reduced as a world power, exactly the way, and at the same degree of speed, that England has been forced to relinquish her Empire. (It is simply not true—and the state of her ex-colonies proves this—that England "always meant to go.") If the states were Southern states—and the Muslims seem to favor this—then the borders of a hostile Latin America would be raised, in effect, to, say, Maryland. Of the American borders on the sea, one would face toward a powerless Europe and the other toward an untrustworthy and non-white East, and on the North, after Canada, there would be only Alaska, which is a Russian border. The effect of this would be that the white people of the United States and Canada would find themselves marooned on a hostile continent, with the rest of the white world probably unwilling and certainly unable to come to their aid. All this is not, to my mind, the most imminent of possibilities, but if I were a Muslim, this is the possibility that I would find myself holding in the center of my mind, and driving toward. And if I were a Muslim, I would not hesitate to utilize—or, indeed, to exacerbate—the social and spiritual discontent that reigns here, for, at the very worst, I would merely have contributed to the destruction of a house I hated, and it would not matter if I perished, too. One has been perishing here so long!

And what were they thinking around the table? "I've come," said Elijah, "to give you something which can never be taken away from you." How solemn the table became then, and how great a light rose in the dark faces! This is the message that has spread through streets and tenements and prisons, through the narcotics wards, and past the filth and sadism of mental hospitals to a people from whom everything has been taken away, including, most crucially, their sense of their own worth. People cannot live without this sense; they will do anything whatever to regain it. This is why the most dangerous creation of any soicety is that man who has nothing to lose. You do not need ten such men —one will do. And Elijah, I should imagine, has had nothing to lose since the day he saw his father's blood rush out—rush down, and splash, so the legend has it, down through the leaves of a tree, on him. But neither did the other men around the table have anything to lose. "Return to your true religion," Elijah has written. "Throw off the chains of the slavemaster, the devil, and return to the fold. Stop drinking his alcohol, using his dope—protect your women—and forsake the filthy swine." I remembered my buddies of years ago, in the hallways, with their wine and their whiskey and their tears; in hallways still, frozen on the needle; and my brother saying to me once, "If Harlem didn't have so many churches and junkies, there'd be blood flowing in the streets." *Protect your women:* a difficult thing to do in a civilization sexually so pathetic that the white man's masculinity depends on a denial of the masculinity of the blacks. *Protect your women:* in a civilization that emasculates the male and abuses the female, and in which, moreover, the male is forced to depend on the female's bread-winning power. *Protect your women:* in the teeth of the white man's boast "We figure we're doing you folks a favor by pumping some white blood into your kids," and while facing the Southern shotgun and the Northern billy. Years ago, we used to say, *"Yes, I'm black, goddammit, and I'm beautiful!"*—in defiance, into the void. But now—now—African kings and heroes have come into the world, out of the past, the past that can now be put to the uses of power. And black has *become* a beautiful color—not because it is loved but because it is feared. And this urgency on the part of American Negroes is *not to be forgotten!* As they watch black men elsewhere rise, the promise held out, at last, that they may walk the earth with the authority with which white men walk, protected by the power that white men shall have no longer, is enough, and more than enough, to empty prisons and pull God down from Heaven. It has happened before, many times, before color was invented, and the hope of Heaven has always been a metaphor for the achievement of this particular state of grace. The song says, "I know my robe's going to fit me well. I tried it on at the gates of Hell."

It was time to leave, and we stood in the large living room, saying good night, with everything curiously and heavily unresolved. I could not help feeling that I had failed a test, in their eyes and in my own, or that I had failed to heed a warning. Elijah and I shook hands, and he asked me where I was going. Wherever it was, I would be driven there—"because, when we invite someone here," he said, "we take the responsibility of protecting him from the white devils until he gets wherever it is he's going." I was, in fact, going to have a drink with several white devils on the other side of town. I confess that for a fraction of a second I hesitated to give the address—the kind of address that in Chicago, as in all American cities, identified itself as a white address by virtue of its location. But I did give it, and Elijah and I walked out onto the steps, and one of the young men vanished to get the car. It was very strange to stand with Elijah for those few moments, facing those vivid, violent, so problematical streets. I felt very close to him, and really wished to be able to love and honor him as a witness, an ally, and a father. I felt that I knew something of his pain and his fury, and, yes, even his beauty. Yet precisely because of the reality and the nature of those streets—because of what he conceived as his responsibility and what I took to be mine—we would always be strangers, and possibly, one day, enemies. The car arrived— a gleaming, metallic, grossly American blue—and Elijah and I shook hands and said good night once more. He walked into his mansion and shut the door.

The driver and I started on our way through dark, murmuring—and, at this hour, strangely beautiful—Chicago, along the lake. We returned to the discussion of the land. How were we—Negroes— to get this land? I asked this of the dark boy who had said earlier, at the table, that the white man's actions proved him to be a devil. He spoke to me first of the Muslim temples that were being built, or were about to be built, in various parts of the United States, of the strength of the Muslim following, and of the amount of money that is annually at the disposal of Negroes—something like twenty billion dollars. "That alone shows you how strong we are," he said. But, I persisted, cautiously, and in somewhat different terms, this twenty billion dollars, or whatever it is, depends on the total economy of the United States. What happens when the Negro is no longer a part of this economy? Leaving aside the fact that in order for this to happen the economy of the United States will itself have had to undergo radical and certainly disastrous changes, the American Negro's spending power will obviously no longer be the same. On what, then, will the economy of this separate nation be based? The boy gave me a rather strange look. I said hurriedly, "I'm not saying it *can't* be done—I just want to know *how* it's to be done." I was thinking, In order for this to happen, your entire frame of reference will have to change, and you will be forced to surrender many things that you now scarcely know you have. I didn't feel that the things I had in mind, such as the pseudo-elegant heap of tin in which we were riding, had any very great value. But life would be very different without them, and I wondered if he had thought of this.

How can one, however, dream of power in any other terms than in the symbols of power? The boy could see that freedom depended on the possession of land; he was persuaded that, in one way or another, Negroes must achieve this possession. In the meantime, he could walk the streets and fear nothing, because there were millions like him, coming soon, now, to power. He was held together, in short, by a dream—though it is just as well to remember that some dreams come true—and was united with his "brothers" on the basis of their color. Perhaps one cannot ask for more. People always seem to band together in accordance to a principle that has nothing to do with love, a principle that releases them from personal responsibility.

Yet I could have hoped that the Muslim movement had been able to inculcate in the demoralized Negro population a truer and more individual sense of its own worth, so that Negroes in the Northern ghettos could begin, in concrete terms, and at whatever price, to change their situation. But in order to change a situation one has first to see it for what it is: in the present case, to accept the fact, whatever one does with it thereafter, that the Negro has been formed by this nation, for better or for worse, and does not belong to any other—not to Africa, and certainly not to Islam. The paradox—and a fearful paradox it is—is that the American Negro can have no future anywhere, on any continent, as long as he is unwilling to accept his past. To accept one's past—one's history—is not the same thing as drowning in it; it is learning how to use it. An invented past can never be used; it cracks and crumbles under the pressures of life like clay in a season of drought. How can the American Negro's past be used? The unprecedented price demanded—and at this embattled hour of the world's history—is the transcendence of the realities of color, of nations, and of altars.

"Anyway," the boy said suddenly, after a very long silence, "things won't ever again be the way they used to be. I know *that*."

And so we arrived in enemy territory, and they set me down at the enemy's door.

N O ONE SEEMS to know where the Nation of Islam gets its money. A vast amount, of course, is contributed by Negroes, but there are rumors to the effect that people like Birchites and certain Texas oil millionaires look with favor on the movement. I have no way of knowing whether there is any truth to the rumors, though since these people make such a point of keeping the races separate, I wouldn't be surprised if for this smoke there was some fire. In any case, during a recent Muslim rally, George Lincoln Rockwell, the chief of the American Nazi party, made a point of contributing about twenty dollars to the cause, and he and Malcolm X decided that, racially speaking, anyway, they were in complete agreement. The glorification of one race and the consequent debasement of another—or others—always has been and always will be a recipe for murder. There is no way around this. If one is permitted to treat any group

of people with special disfavor because of their race
or the color of their skin, there is no limit to what
one will force them to endure, and, since the entire
race has been mysteriously indicted, no reason not
to attempt to destroy it root and branch. This is
precisely what the Nazis attempted. Their only
originality lay in the means they used. It is scarcely
worthwhile to attempt remembering how many
times the sun has looked down on the slaughter of
the innocents. I am very much concerned that
American Negroes achieve their freedom here in
the United States. But I am also concerned for their
dignity, for the health of their souls, and must oppose any attempt that Negroes may make to do
to others what has been done to them. I think I
know—we see it around us every day—the spiritual
wasteland to which that road leads. It is so simple
a fact and one that is so hard, apparently, to grasp:
Whoever debases others is debasing himself. That
is not a mystical statement but a most realistic one,
which is proved by the eyes of any Alabama sheriff
—and I would not like to see Negroes ever arrive
at so wretched a condition.

Now, it is extremely unlikely that Negroes will
ever rise to power in the United States, because
they are only approximately a ninth of this nation.
They are not in the position of the Africans, who

are attempting to reclaim their land and break the colonial yoke and recover from the colonial experience. The Negro situation is dangerous in a different way, both for the Negro qua Negro and for the country of which he forms so troubled and troubling a part. The American Negro is a unique creation; he has no counterpart anywhere, and no predecessors. The Muslims react to this fact by referring to the Negro as "the so-called American Negro" and substituting for the names inherited from slavery the letter "X." It is a fact that every American Negro bears a name that originally belonged to the white man whose chattel he was. I am called Baldwin because I was either sold by my African tribe or kidnapped out of it into the hands of a white Christian named Baldwin, who forced me to kneel at the foot of the cross. I am, then, both visibly and legally the descendant of slaves in a white, Protestant country, and this is what it means to be an American Negro, this is who he is—a kidnapped pagan, who was sold like an animal and treated like one, who was once defined by the American Constitution as "three-fifths" of a man, and who, according to the Dred Scott decision, had no rights that a white man was bound to respect. And today, a hundred years after his technical emancipation, he remains—with the possible exception of the American Indian—the most despised creature in his country. Now, there is simply no possibility of a real change in the Negro's situation without the most radical and far-reaching changes in the American political and social structure. And it is clear that white Americans are not simply unwilling to effect these changes; they are, in the main, so slothful have they become, unable even to envision them. It must be added that the Negro himself no longer believes in the good faith of white Americans—if, indeed, he ever could have. What the Negro *has* discovered, and on an international level, is that power to intimidate which he has always had privately but hitherto could manipulate only privately—for private ends often, for limited ends always. And therefore when the country speaks of a "new" Negro, which it has been doing every hour on the hour for decades, it is not really referring to a change in the Negro, which, in any case, it is quite incapable of assessing, but only to a new difficulty in keeping him in his place, to the fact that it encounters him (again! again!) barring yet another door to its spiritual and social ease. This is probably, hard and odd as it may sound, the most important thing that one human being can do for another—it is certainly *one* of the most important things; hence the torment and necessity of love—and this is the enormous contribution that the Negro has made to this otherwise shapeless and undiscovered country. Consequently, white Americans are in nothing more deluded than in supposing that Negroes could ever have imagined that white people would "give" them anything. It is rare indeed that people give. Most people guard and keep; they suppose that it is they themselves and what they identify with themselves that they are guarding and keeping, whereas what they are actually guarding and keeping is their system of reality and what they assume themselves to be. One can give nothing whatever without giving oneself—that is to say, risking oneself. If one cannot risk oneself, then one is simply incapable of giving. And, after all, one can give freedom only by setting someone free. This, in the case of the Negro, the American republic has never become sufficiently mature to do. White Americans have contented themselves with gestures that are now described as "tokenism." For hard example, white Americans congratulate themselves on the 1954 Supreme Court decision outlawing segregation in the schools; they suppose, in spite of the mountain of evidence that has since accumulated to the contrary, that this was proof of a change of heart—or, as they like to say, progress. Perhaps. It all depends on how one reads the word "progress." Most of the Negroes I know do not believe that this immense concession would ever have been made if it had not been for the competition of the Cold War, and the fact that Africa was clearly liberating herself and therefore had, for political reasons, to be wooed by the descendants of her former masters. Had it been a matter of love or justice, the 1954 decision would surely have occurred sooner; were it not for the realities of power in this difficult era, it might very well not have occurred yet. This seems an extremely harsh way of stating the case—ungrateful, as it were—but the evidence that supports this way of stating it is not easily refuted. I myself do not think that it can be refuted at all. In any event, the sloppy and fatuous nature of American good will can never be relied upon to deal with hard problems. These have been dealt with, when they have been dealt with at all, out of necessity—and in political terms, anyway, necessity means concessions made in order to stay on top. I think this is a fact, which it serves no purpose to deny, *but, whether it is a fact or not, this is what the black population of the world, including black Americans, really believe.* The word "independence" in Africa and the word "integration" here are almost equally meaningless; that is, Europe has not yet left Africa, and black men here are not yet free. And both of these last statements are undeniable facts, related facts, containing the gravest implications for us all. The Negroes of this country may never be able to rise to power, but they are very well placed indeed to precipitate chaos and ring down the curtain on the American dream.

This has everything to do, of course, with the nature of that dream and with the fact that we Americans, of whatever color, do not dare examine it and are far from having made it a reality. There are too many things we do not wish to know about ourselves. People are not, for example, terribly anxious to be equal (equal, after all, to what and to whom?) but they love the idea of being superior. And this human truth has an especially grinding force here, where identity is almost impossible to achieve and people are perpetually attempting to find their feet on the shifting sands of status. (Consider the history of labor in a country in which, spiritually speaking, there are no workers, only candidates for the hand of the boss's daughter.) Furthermore, I have met only a very few people—and most of these were not Americans—who had any real desire to be free. Freedom is hard to bear. It can be objected that I am speaking of political freedom in spiritual terms, but the political institutions of any nation are always menaced and are ultimately controlled by the spiritual state of that nation. We are controlled here by our confusion, far more than we know, and the American dream has therefore become something much more closely resembling a nightmare, on the private, domestic, and international levels. Privately, we cannot stand our lives and dare not examine them; domestically, we take no responsibility for (and no pride in) what goes on in our country; and, internationally, for many millions of people, we are an unmitigated disaster. Whoever doubts this last statement has only to open his ears, his heart, his mind, to the testimony of—for example—any Cuban peasant or any Spanish poet, and ask himself what *he* would feel about us if *he* were the victim of our performance in pre-Castro Cuba or in Spain. We defend our curious role in Spain by referring to the Russian menace and the necessity of protecting the free world. It has not occurred to us that we have simply been mesmerized by Russia, and that the only real advantage Russia has in what we think of as a struggle between the East and the West is the moral history of the Western world. Russia's secret weapon is the bewilderment and despair and hunger of millions of people of whose existence we are scarcely aware. The Russian Communists are not in the least concerned about these people. But our ignorance and indecision have had the effect, if not of delivering them into Russian hands, of plunging them very deeply in the Russian shadow, for which effect—and it is hard to blame them—the most articulate among them, and the most oppressed as well, distrust us all the more. Our power and our fear of change help bind these people to their misery and bewilderment, and insofar as they find this state intolerable we are intolerably menaced. For if they find their state intolerable, but are too heavily oppressed to change it, they are simply pawns in the hands of larger powers, which, in such a context, are always unscrupulous, and when, eventually, they do change their situation—as in Cuba—we are menaced more than ever, by the vacuum that succeeds all violent upheavals. We should certainly know by now that it is one thing to overthrow a dictator or repel an invader and quite another thing really to achieve a revolution. Time and time and time again, the people discover that they have merely betrayed themselves into the hands of yet another Pharaoh, who, since he was necessary to put the broken country together, will not let them go. Perhaps, people being the conundrums that they are, and having so little desire to shoulder the burden of their lives, this is what will always happen. But at the bottom of my heart I do not believe this. I think that people can be better than that, and I know that people can be better than they are. We are capable of bearing a great burden, once we discover that the burden is reality and arrive where reality is. Anyway, the point here is that we are living in an age of revolution, whether we will or no, and that America is the only Western nation with both the power and, as I hope to suggest, the experience that may help to make these revolutions real and minimize the human damage. Any attempt we make to oppose these outbursts of energy is tantamount to signing our death warrant.

Behind what we think of as the Russian menace lies what we do not wish to face, and what white Americans do not face when they regard a Negro: reality—the fact that life is tragic. Life is tragic simply because the earth turns and the sun inexorably rises and sets, and one day, for each of us, the sun will go down for the last, last time. Perhaps the whole root of our trouble, the human trouble, is that we will sacrifice all the beauty of our lives, will imprison ourselves in totems, taboos, crosses, blood sacrifices, steeples, mosques, races, armies, flags, nations, in order to deny the fact of death, which is the only fact we have. It seems to me that one ought to rejoice in the *fact* of death—ought to decide, indeed, to *earn* one's death by confronting with passion the conundrum of life. One is responsible to life: It is the small beacon in that terrifying darkness from which we come and to which we shall return. One must negotiate this passage as nobly as possible, for the sake of those who are coming after us. But white Americans do not believe in death, and this is why the darkness of my skin so intimidates them. And this is also why the presence of the Negro in this country can bring about its destruction. It is the responsibility of free men to trust and to celebrate what is constant—birth, struggle, and death are constant, and so is love, though we may not always think so—and to apprehend the nature of change, to be able and willing to change. I speak of change not on the surface but in the depths—change in the sense of renewal. But renewal becomes impossible if one supposes things to be constant that are not—safety, for example, or money, or power. One clings then to chimeras, by which one can only be betrayed, and the entire hope—the entire possibility—of freedom disappears. And by destruction I mean precisely the abdication by Americans of any effort really to be free. The Negro can precipitate this abdication because white Americans have never, in all their long history. been able to look on him as a man like themselves. This point need not be labored; it is proved over and over again by the Negro's continuing position here, and his indescribable struggle to defeat the stratagems that white Americans have used, and use, to deny him his humanity. America could have used in other ways the energy that both groups have expended in this conflict. America, of all the Western nations, has been best placed to prove the uselessness and the obsolescence of the concept of color. But it has not dared to accept this opportunity, or even to conceive of it as an opportunity. White Americans have thought of it as their shame, and have envied those more civilized and elegant European nations that were untroubled by the presence of black men on their shores. This is because white Americans have supposed "Europe" and "civilization" to be synonyms—which they are not—and have been distrustful of other standards and other sources of vitality, especially those produced in America itself, and have attempted to behave in all matters as though what was east for Europe was also east for them. What it comes to is that if we, who can scarcely be considered a white nation, persist in thinking of ourselves as one, we condemn ourselves, with the truly white nations, to sterility and decay, whereas if we could accept ourselves *as we are*, we might bring new life to the Western achievements, and transform them. The price of this transformation is the unconditional freedom of the Negro; it is not too much to say that he, who has been so long rejected, must now be embraced, and at no matter what psychic or social risk. He is *the* key figure in his country, and the American future is precisely as bright or as dark as his. And the Negro recognizes this, in a negative way. Hence the question: Do I really *want* to be integrated into a burning house?

White Americans find it as difficult as white people elsewhere do to divest themselves of the notion that they are in possession of some intrinsic value that black people need, or want. And this assumption—which, for example, makes the solution to the Negro problem depend on the speed with which Negroes accept and adopt white standards—is revealed in all kinds of striking ways, from Bobby Kennedy's assurance that a Negro can become President in forty years to the unfortunate tone of warm congratulation with which so many liberals address their Negro equals. It is the Negro, of course, who is presumed to have become equal—an achievement that not only proves the comforting fact that perseverance has no color but also overwhelmingly corroborates the white man's sense of his own value. Alas, this value can scarcely be corroborated in any other way; there is certainly little enough in the white man's public or private life that one should desire to imitate. White men, at the bottom of their hearts, know this. Therefore, a vast amount of the energy that goes into what we call the Negro problem is produced by the white man's profound desire not to be judged by those who are not white, not to be seen as he is, and at the same time a vast amount of the white anguish is rooted in the white man's equally profound need to be seen as he is, to be released from the tyranny of his mirror. All of us know, whether or not we are able to admit it, that mirrors can only lie, that death by drowning is all that awaits one there. It is for this reason that love is so desperately sought and so cunningly avoided. Love takes off the masks that we fear we cannot live without and know we cannot live within. I use the word "love" here not merely in the personal sense but as a state of being, or a state of grace—not in the infantile American sense of being made happy but in the tough and universal sense of quest and daring and growth. And I submit, then, that the racial tensions that menace Americans today have little to do with real antipathy—on the contrary, indeed—and are involved only symbolically with color. These tensions are rooted in the very same depths as those from which love springs, or murder. The white man's unadmitted—and apparently, to him, unspeakable—private fears and longings are projected onto the Negro. The only way he can be released from the Negro's tyrannical power over him is to consent, in effect, to become black himself, to become a part of that suffering and dancing country that he now watches wistfully from the heights of his lonely power and, armed with spiritual traveller's checks, visits surreptitiously after dark. How can one respect, let alone adopt, the values of a people who do not, on any level whatever, live the way they say they do, or the way they say they should? I cannot accept the proposition that the four-hundred-year travail of the American Negro should result merely in his attainment of the present level of the American civilization. I am far from convinced that being released from the African witch doctor was worthwhile if I am now—in order to support the moral contradictions and the spiritual aridity of my life—expected to become dependent on the American psychiatrist. It is a bargain I refuse. The only thing white people have that black people need, or should want, is power—and no one holds power forever. White people cannot, in the generality, be taken as models of how to live. Rather, the white man is

himself in sore need of new standards, which will
release him from his confusion and place him once
again in fruitful communion with the depths of his
own being. And I repeat: The price of the liberation of the white people is the liberation of the
blacks—the total liberation, in the cities, in the
towns, before the law, and in the mind. Why, for
example—especially knowing the family as I do—
I should *want* to marry your sister is a great mystery
to me. But your sister and I have every right to
marry if we wish to, and no one has the right to
stop us. If she cannot raise me to her level, perhaps
I can raise her to mine.

In short, we, the black and the white, deeply
need each other here if we are really to become a
nation—if we are really, that is, to achieve our
identity, our maturity, as men and women. To
create one nation has proved to be a hideously
difficult task; there is certainly no need now to
create two, one black and one white. But white
men with far more political power than that
possessed by the Nation of Islam movement have
been advocating exactly this, in effect, for generations. If this sentiment is honored when it falls from
the lips of Senator Byrd, then there is no reason it
should not be honored when it falls from the lips
of Malcolm X. And any Congressional committee

wishing to investigate the latter must also be willing to investigate the former. They are expressing exactly the same sentiments and represent exactly the same danger. There is absolutely no reason to suppose that white people are better equipped to frame the laws by which I am to be governed than I am. It is entirely unacceptable that I should have no voice in the political affairs of my own country, for I am not a ward of America; I am one of the first Americans to arrive on these shores.

This past, the Negro's past, of rope, fire, torture, castration, infanticide, rape; death and humiliation; fear by day and night, fear as deep as the marrow of the bone; doubt that he was worthy of life, since everyone around him denied it; sorrow for his women, for his kinfolk, for his children, who needed his protection, and whom he could not protect; rage, hatred, and murder, hatred for white men so deep that it often turned against him and his own, and made all love, all trust, all joy impossible—this past, this endless struggle to achieve and reveal and confirm a human identity, human authority, yet contains, for all its horror, something very beautiful. I do not mean to be sentimental about suffering—enough is certainly as good as a feast—but people who cannot suffer can never grow up, can never discover who they are. That man who is forced each day to snatch his manhood, his identity, out of the fire of human cruelty that rages to destroy it knows, if he survives his effort, and even if he does not survive it, something about himself and human life that no school on earth—and, indeed, no church—can teach. He achieves his own authority, and that is unshakable. This is because, in order to save his life, he is forced to look beneath appearances, to take nothing for granted, to hear the meaning behind the words. If one is continually surviving the worst that life can bring, one eventually ceases to be controlled by a fear of what life can bring; whatever it brings must be borne. And at this level of experience one's bitterness begins to be palatable, and hatred becomes too heavy a sack to carry. The apprehension of life here so briefly and inadequately sketched has been the experience of generations of Negroes, and it helps to explain how they have endured and how they have been able to produce children of kindergarten age who can walk through mobs to get to school. It demands great force and great cunning continually to assault the mighty and indifferent fortress of white supremacy, as Negroes in this country have done so long. It demands great spiritual resilience not to hate the hater whose foot is on your neck, and an even greater miracle of perception and charity not to teach your child to hate. The Negro boys and girls who are facing mobs today come out of a long line of improbable aristocrats—the only genuine aristocrats this country has produced. I say "this country" because their frame of reference was totally American. They were hewing out of the mountain of white supremacy the stone of their individuality. I have great respect for that unsung army of black men and women who trudged down back lanes and entered back doors, saying "Yes, sir" and "No, Ma'am" in order to acquire a new roof for the schoolhouse, new books, a new chemistry lab, more beds for the dormitories, more dormitories. They did not like saying "Yes, sir" and "No Ma'am," but the country was in no hurry to educate Negroes, these black men and women knew that the job had to be done, and they put their pride in their pockets in order to do it. It is very hard to believe that they were in any way inferior to the white men and women who opened those back doors. It is very hard to believe that those men and women, raising their children, eating their greens, crying their curses, weeping their tears, singing their songs, making their love, as the sun rose, as the sun set, were in any way inferior to the white men and women who crept over to share these splendors after the sun went down. But we must avoid the European error; we must not suppose that, because the situation, the ways, the perceptions of black people so radically differed from those of whites, they were racially superior. I am proud of these people not because of their color but because of their intelligence and their spiritual force and their beauty. The country should be proud of them, too, but, alas, not many people in this country even know of their existence. And the reason for this ignorance is that a knowledge of the role these people played—and play—in American life would reveal more about America to Americans than Americans wish to know.

The American Negro has the great advantage of having never believed that collection of myths to which white Americans cling: that their ancestors were all freedom-loving heroes, that they were born in the greatest country the world has ever seen, or that Americans are invincible in battle and wise in peace, that Americans have always dealt honorably with Mexicans and Indians and all other neighbors or inferiors, that American men are the world's most direct and virile, that American women are pure. Negroes know far more about white Americans than that; it can almost be said, in fact, that they know about white Americans what parents—or, anyway, mothers—know about their children, and that they very often regard white Americans that way. And perhaps this attitude, held in spite of what they know and have endured, helps to explain why Negroes, on the whole, and until lately, have allowed themselves to feel so little hatred. The tendency has really been, insofar as this was possible, to dismiss white people as the slightly mad victims of their own brainwashing. One watched the lives they led. One could not be fooled about that; one watched the things they did and the excuses that they gave themselves, and if a white man was really in trouble, deep trouble, it was to the Negro's door that he came. And one felt that if one had had that white man's worldly advantages, one would never have become as bewildered and as joyless and as thoughtlessly cruel as he. The Negro came to the white man for a roof or for five dollars or for a letter to the judge; the white man came to the Negro for love. But he was not often able to give what he came seeking. The price was too high; he had too much to lose. And the Negro knew this, too. When one knows this about a man, it is impossible for one to hate him, but unless he becomes a man—becomes equal—it is also impossible for one to love him. Ultimately, one tends to avoid him, for the universal characteristic of children is to assume that they have a monopoly on trouble, and therefore a monopoly on *you*. (Ask any Negro what he knows about the white people with whom he works. And then ask the white people with whom he works what they know about *him*.)

How can the American Negro past be used? It is entirely possible that this dishonored past will rise up soon to smite all of us. There are some wars, for example (if anyone on the globe is still mad enough to go to war) that the American Negro will not support, however many of his people may be coerced—and there is a limit to the number of people any government can put in prison, and a rigid limit indeed to the practicality of such a course. A bill is coming in that I fear America is not prepared to pay. "The problem of the twentieth century," wrote W. E. B. Du Bois around sixty years ago, "is the problem of the color line." A fearful and delicate problem, which compromises, when it does not corrupt, all the American efforts to build a better world—here, there, or anywhere. It is for this reason that everything white Americans think they believe in must now be reëxamined. What one would not like to see again is the consolidation of peoples on the basis of their color. But as long as we in the West place on color the value that we do, we make it impossible for the great unwashed to consolidate themselves according to any other principle. Color is not a human or a personal reality; it is a political reality. But this is a distinction so extremely hard to make that the West has not been able to make it yet. And at the center of this dreadful storm, this vast confusion, stand the black people of this nation, who must now share the fate of a nation that has never accepted them, to which they were brought in chains. Well, if this is so, one has no choice but to do all in one's power to change that fate, and at no matter what risk—eviction, imprisonment, torture, death. For the sake of one's children, in order to minimize the bill that *they* must pay, one must be careful not to take refuge in any delusion—and the value placed on the color of the skin is always and everywhere and forever a delusion. I know that what I am asking is impossible. But in our time, as in every time, the impossible is the least that one can demand—and one is, after all, emboldened by the spectacle of human history in general, and American Negro history in particular, for it testifies to nothing less than the perpetual achievement of the impossible.

When I was very young, and was dealing with my buddies in those wine- and urine-stained hallways, something in me wondered, *What will happen to all that beauty?* For black people, though I am aware that some of us, black and white, do not know it yet, are very beautiful. And when I sat at Elijah's table and watched the baby, the women, and the men, and we talked about God's—or Allah's —vengeance, I wondered, when that vengeance was achieved, *What will happen to all that beauty then?* I could also see that the intransigence and ignorance of the white world might make that vengeance inevitable—a vengeance that does not really depend on, and cannot really be executed by, any person or organization, and that cannot be prevented by any police force or army: historical vengeance, a cosmic vengeance, based on the law that we recognize when we say, "Whatever goes up must come down." And here we are, at the center of the arc, trapped in the gaudiest, most valuable, and most improbable water wheel the world has ever seen. Everything now, we must assume, is in our hands; we have no right to assume otherwise. If we—and now I mean the relatively conscious whites and the relatively conscious blacks, who must, like lovers, insist on, or create, the consciousness of the others—do not falter in our duty now, we may be able, handful that we are, to end the racial nightmare, and achieve our country, and change the history of the world. If we do not now dare everything, the fulfillment of that prophecy, re-created from the Bible in song by a slave, is upon us: *God gave Noah the rainbow sign, No more water, the fire next time!*

CONNECTIONS

Burn, Baby, Burn

Jimmy Collier

Middle of the summer, bitten by flies and fleas,
Sittin' in a crowded apartment, about a-hundred-and-
    ten degrees,
I went outside, the middle of the night
All I had was a match in my hand, but I wanted to fight,
So I said, Burn, baby, burn
        Burn, baby, burn
        Nowhere to be, and-a no one to see,
        I said-a nowhere to turn
        Burn, baby, burn.

I called President Johnson[1] on the phone,
The secretary said he wasn't there
I tried to get in touch with Mr. Humphrey[2]
They couldn't find him anywhere.
I went into the courtroom, with my poor sad face
Didn't have no money, didn't have no lawyer
They wouldn't plead my case
So I said, Burn, baby, burn
        Burn, baby, burn
        Nowhere to be, and-a no one to see,
        I said-a nowhere to turn
        Burn, baby, burn.

---

1. Lyndon Baines Johnson (1908–1973), 36th President of the United States
(1963–1969).
2. Hubert H. Humphrey (1911–1978), Vice President of the United States
(1965–1969).

I really wanted a decent job, I really needed some scratch
    (I heard people talking about a dream, now, a
    dream that I couldn't catch)
I really wanted to be somebody and all I had was a match
Couldn't get oil from Rockefeller's wells
Couldn't get diamonds from the mine
If I can't enjoy the American dream, won't be water but
    fire next time
So I said, Burn, baby, burn
        Burn, baby, burn
        Nowhere to be, and-a no one to see,
        I said-a nowhere to turn
        Burn, baby, burn.

Walkin' around on the west side now, lookin' mean and
    mad
Deep down inside my heart, I'm feeling sorry and sad
Got a knife and a razor blade, everybody that I know is
    tough,
But when I tried to burn my way out of the ghetto,
I burned my own self up, when I said,
        Burn, baby, burn
        Burn, baby, burn
        Nowhere to be, and-a no one to see,
        I said-a nowhere to turn
        Burn, baby, burn.

Learn, baby, learn
Learn, baby, learn
You need a concern
You've got money to earn
You've got midnight oil to burn, baby, burn.

I really want a decent education, I really want a decent
    place to stay
I really want some decent clothes, now,
I really want a decent family
I really want a decent life like everybody else. . . .

*"I made up this song while the riot in Watts was going on. I
was searching for ways to try and express what I thought these
fellows in Watts were trying to say by burning the town down.*

*We're trying to work with these same type fellows here
in Chicago. Most of them think the Movement is kinda
square. Their attitude is 'let's tear this town up.' They spend
part of their time beating up white people and it's bad
because this violence is becoming institutionalized. It's not
their fault. It's the fault of the system, because you've got
Negro guys growing up now who've never had good experiences with white people, and their families have never had
good experiences with white people.*

But now Orange works out with some of them in
karate and judo and he can lick 'em all, so they respect his
ideas about non-violence.*

*And with this song, part way through, after they've
sung the song and got out some of their hate and some of*

---

*James Orange—six feet, three inches, 280 lbs.—is a veteran of Alabama
and other southern movements.

*their vengeance, we try to put in our own pitch about using
non-violence to change things. We say you've got to learn,
baby, learn, and what you really want to do is build something rather than tear down."*

                                                    Jimmy Collier

■   ■   ■

Whatever is Necessary to Protect Ourselves

Les Crane Interview, December 2, 1964

from *Malcolm X: The Last Speeches*

LES CRANE: My next guest is Mr. Malcolm X, ladies and gentlemen. [*Applause*]

This interview is going to be a little difficult for me to do, because I know Malcolm. We've done shows together before. He's been a guest of mine on a couple of different occasions. We've had telephone conversations of length and interest. And—so to get the story, I'm going to make believe that we've never met, okay?

Malcolm X: That's fine. That's the best way.

Crane: All right. Let's start from the beginning. First of all, what is the Black Muslim movement?

Malcolm X: Well, as you know, I'm not in the Black Muslim movement. But the Black Muslim movement is an organization in this country that's headed by Elijah Muhammad.

Crane: That's all?

Malcolm X: It's an organization that's headed by Elijah Muhammad. It says it's a religious organization and that its religion is Islam. But the people in the world of Islam don't accept it as an orthodox Islamic religious organization.

Crane: In other words, they claim to be a branch, an American branch, of the Muhammadan religion.

Malcolm X: No, not the Muhammadan. The real Muslim never refers to his religion as the Muhammadan religion. His religion is Islam.

Crane: Muhammad being the prophet of that—

Malcolm X: Muhammad is one of the prophets of that religion. The people who believe in that religion believe in all of the prophets—Moses, Abraham, Jesus, all of them. But they believe in Muhammad ibn Abd Allah as the last of the prophets. And Elijah Muhammad in this country says that he is also teaching that religion. But that religion is a religion of brotherhood. It advocates the brotherhood of man, all men—

Crane: That's the Muslim religion?

Malcolm X: Yes. This is the—well, those who practice the religion of Islam call themselves Muslims. In this country they're referred to as Moslems.

Crane: Now, you consider yourself to be a Moslem in this country—

Malcolm X: I'm a Moslem. I believe in the religion of Islam.

Crane: And you are no longer a member of the Black Muslims?

Malcolm X: No, no.

Crane: Now what caused that split?

Malcolm X: Well actually, I don't think that it's any—that it contributes anything constructive to go into what caused the split. I'm not in it. I was inseparable from it while I was in it. But now I'm not. I leave it in the past.

Crane: Well, I don't know how valuable it would be—you know, it was inconceivable to think of the Black Muslim movement in this country without thinking of Malcolm X. You were Elijah Muhammad's right-hand man and his leading spokesman, as well as the head of the mosque in New York, which is the largest Black Muslim mosque in the country, as I understood it. And there were certain things that the Black Muslims represented, at least in my mind through your speeches, that I think are worthy of discussion.

Malcolm X: Well, yes. I represented him probably more diligently than all of the rest of his representatives combined. And this somewhat led to the eventual split. Human nature being what it is—

Crane: Sort of like a power play almost?

Malcolm X: Human nature being what it is.

Crane: Call it politics. We'll call it that.

Malcolm X: Yes.

Crane: But also you said that your trip to Africa has changed your thinking and your position to a great extent.

Malcolm X: Yes. One thing—travel always broadens one's scope. Travel does. . . . Twice this year I visited both Africa and the Middle East. The first time I went was in April and May. I went to Mecca. I went primarily to get a better understanding of Islam.

There were things that happened between me and Elijah Muhammad that caused me to greatly question his ability as a man, much less as a religious leader. And, based upon that doubt, I went in search of an understanding of the religion of Islam. I made the *hajj* or the pilgrimage to Mecca. While I was—one of the things that Elijah Muhammad always taught us was that Islam is a religion of God. It was a religion in which no whites could participate. And he used—to prove his point, he told us that Mecca was a forbidden city. A city that was forbidden to non-Muslims. And since a white person couldn't be a Muslim in his teaching, he said that no white could enter Mecca.

Well, I went to Mecca in May—rather, in April—and everyone was there. In fact one member of the Turkish parliament, who had brought busloads, several hundred busloads, from Turkey to make the pilgrimage, was standing with me on the steps of the hotel in Mina, which is a short distance from Mecca. And he pointed out at that time that Mecca, during the *hajj* season, or the pilgrimage season, would be an anthropologist's paradise, because every specimen of humanity is represented there. It's an absolute brotherhood. So that when I saw this with my own eyes, and saw that people of all colors could practice brotherhood, it was at that point that I wrote back and pointed out that I believed in Islam as a religion of brotherhood.

But this belief in brotherhood doesn't alter the fact that I'm also an Afro-American, or American Negro as you wish, in a society which has very serious and severe race problems which no religion can blind me to.

Crane: Well, what's interesting to me, there are words that you never used to use in the past in our discussions. You never used to use the word *Negro.* That word offended you. You used to say "the so-called Negro"—

Malcolm X: Well, I said Afro-American or American Negro, as you will—

Crane: And you believed also that brotherhood was impossible at one point—

Malcolm X: Let me explain. The reason I say—
Afro-American is a term that our people in this country

increasingly are beginning to use to identify themselves. But in using it, I take into consideration that many people don't know what is meant by Afro-American, so I use the word *Negro* to let you know I was still talking about us. . . .

Crane: Integration offends you. You don't believe in the use of that word. You prefer to think of it as brotherhood which is, for the purposes of our discussion, going to be the same thing. But in the old days you didn't believe in brotherhood, you believed in pure strict separation, didn't you?

Malcolm X: Whenever I opened my mouth, I always said that Elijah Muha—the Honorable Elijah Muhammad—teaches us thus and so. And I spoke for him. I represented him. I represented an organization and organizational thinking. Many of my own views that I had from personal experience I kept to myself. I was faithful to that organization and to that man. Since things came about that made me doubt his integrity, I thought—I think for myself, I listen as much as I can to everyone and try and come up with a capsule opinion, capsulized opinion.

I believe that it is possible for brotherhood to be brought about among all people, but I don't delude myself into dreaming or falling for a dream that this exists before it exists. Some of the American—some of the leaders of our people in this country always say that they, you know, they believe in this dream. But while they're dreaming, our people are having a nightmare, and I don't think that you can make a dream come true by pretending that that dream exists when it doesn't.

Crane: You've been a critic of some of the Negro leadership in this country—Martin Luther King, Roy Wilkins, Abernathy, and others—have you changed in your feelings toward them of late?

Malcolm X: I think all of us should be critics of each other. Whenever you can't stand criticism you can never grow. I don't think that it serves any purpose for the leaders of our people to waste their time fighting each other needlessly. I think that we accomplish more when we sit down in private and iron out whatever differences that may exist and try and then do something constructive for the benefit of our people. But on the other hand, I don't think that we should be above criticism. I don't think that anyone should be above criticism.

Crane: Violence or the threat of violence has always surrounded you. Speeches that you've made have been interpreted as being threats. You have made statements reported in the press about how the Negroes should go out and arm themselves, form militias of their own. I read a thing once, a statement I believe you made that every Negro should belong to the National Rifle Association—

Malcolm X: No, I said this: That in areas of this country where the government has proven its—either its inability or its unwillingness to protect the lives and property of our people, then it's only fair to expect us to do whatever is necessary to protect ourselves. And in situations like Mississippi, places like Mississippi where the government actually has proven its inability to protect us—and it has been proven that ofttimes the police officers and sheriffs themselves are involved

in the murder that takes place against our people—
then I feel, and I say that anywhere, that our people
should start doing what is necessary to protect ourselves. This doesn't mean that we should buy rifles
and go out and initiate attacks indiscriminately against
whites. But it does mean that we should get whatever
is necessary to protect ourselves in a country or in an
area where the governmental ability to protect us has
broken down—

Crane: Therefore you do not agree with Dr. King's
Gandhian philosophy—

Malcolm X: My belief in brotherhood would never
restrain me in any way from protecting myself in a
society from a people whose disrespect for brotherhood makes them feel inclined to put my neck on a
tree at the end of a rope. [*Applause*]

Crane: Well, it sounds as though you could be
preaching a sort of an anarchy—

Malcolm X: No, no. I respect government and
respect law. But does the government and the law
respect us? If the FBI, which is what people depend
upon on a national scale to protect the morale and the
property and the lives of the people, can't do so when
the property and lives of Negroes and whites who try
and help Negroes are concerned, then I think that it's
only fair to expect elements to do whatever is necessary to protect themselves.

And this is no departure from normal procedure.
Because right here in New York City you have vigilante
committees that have been set up by groups who see
where their neighborhood community is endangered
and the law can't do anything about it. So—and even

their lives aren't at stake. So—but the fear, Les, seems to come into existence only when someone says Negroes should form vigilante committees to protect their lives and their property.

I'm not advocating the breaking of any laws. But I say that our people will never be respected as human beings until we react as other normal, intelligent human beings do. And this country came into existence by people who were tired of tyranny and oppression and exploitation and the brutality that was being inflicted upon them by powers higher than they, and I think that it is only fair to expect us, sooner or later, to do likewise.

Crane: One last question. You don't preach separatism anymore and I assume you don't want to set up a Black African state in this country anymore. What is your main effort toward now?

Malcolm X: Well, the—one of the organizations which we've now formed, the Organization of Afro-American Unity, has reached the conclusion, after a careful analysis of the problem, that approaching our problem just on the level of civil rights and keeping it within the jurisdiction of the United States will not bring a solution. It's not a Negro problem or an American problem any longer. It's a world problem, it's a human problem. And so we're striving to lift it from the level of civil rights to the level of human rights. And at that level it's international. We can bring it into the United Nations and discuss it in the same tone and in the same language as the problems of people in other parts of the world also is discussed.

Crane: I'm afraid the clock has caught us. It has been interesting. Thank you so much for coming up.
Malcolm X: You're welcome. [*Applause*]

■ ■ ■

Passing

Langston Hughes

Chicago,
Sunday, Oct. 10.

DEAR MA,

I felt like a dog, passing you downtown last night
and not speaking to you. You were great, though. Didn't
give a sign that you even knew me, let alone I was your
son. If I hadn't had the girl with me, Ma, we might
have talked. I'm not as scared as I used to be about
somebody taking me for colored any more just because
I'm seen talking on the street to a Negro. I guess in
looks I'm sort of suspect-proof, anyway. You remember what a hard time I used to have in school trying
to convince teachers I was really colored. Sometimes,
even after they met you, my mother, they wouldn't
believe it. They just thought I had a mulatto mammy,
I guess. Since I've begun to pass for white, nobody has
ever doubted that I am a white man. Where I work,
the boss is a Southerner, and is always cussing out
Negroes in my presence, not dreaming I'm one. It is
to laugh!

Funny thing, though, Ma, how some white people
certainly don't like colored people, do they? (If they
did, then I wouldn't have to be passing to keep my good
job.) They go out of their way sometimes to say bad
things about colored folks, putting it out that all of us
are thieves and liars, or else diseased—consumption
and syphilis, and the like. No wonder it's hard for a

black man to get a good job with that kind of false propaganda going around. I never knew they made a practice of saying such terrible things about us until I started passing and heard their conversations and lived their life.

But I don't mind being "white," Ma, and it was mighty generous of you to urge me to go ahead and make use of my light skin and good hair. It got me this job, Ma, where I still get $65 a week in spite of the depression. And I'm in line for promotion to the chief office secretary, if Mr. Weeks goes to Washington. When I look at the colored boy porter who sweeps out the office, I think that that's what I might be doing if I wasn't light-skinned enough to get by. No matter how smart that boy'd get to be, they wouldn't hire him for a clerk in the office, not if they knew it. Only for a porter. That's why I sometimes get a kick out of putting something over on the boss, who never dreams he's got a colored secretary.

But, Ma, I felt mighty bad about last night. The first time we'd met in public that way. That's the kind of thing that makes passing hard, having to deny your own family when you see them. Of course, I know you and I both realize it is all for the best, but anyhow it's terrible. I love you, Ma, and hate to do it, even if you say you don't mind.

But what did you think of the girl with me, Ma? She's the kid I'm going to marry. Pretty good looking, isn't she? Nice disposition. The parents are well fixed. Her folks are German Americans and don't have much prejudice about them, either. I took her to see a colored revue last week and she thought it was great. She said, "Darkies are so graceful and gay." I wonder what she would have said if I'd told her *I* was colored, or half-colored—that my old man was white, but you weren't? But I guess I won't go into that. Since I've made up my mind to live in the white world, and have found my place in it (a good place), why think about race any more? I'm glad I don't have to, I know that much.

I hope Charlie and Gladys don't feel bad about me. It's funny I was the only one of the kids light enough to pass. Charlie's darker than you, even, Ma. I know he sort of resented it in school when the teachers used to take me for white, before they knew we were brothers. I used to feel bad about it, too, then. But now I'm glad you backed me up, and told me to go ahead and get all I could out of life. That's what I'm going to do, Ma. I'm going to marry white and live white, and if any of my kids are born dark I'll swear they aren't mine. I won't get caught in the mire of color again. Not me. I'm free, Ma, free!

I'd be glad, though, if I could get away from Chicago, transferred to the New York office, or the San Francisco branch of the firm—somewhere where what happened last night couldn't ever occur again. It was awful passing *you* and not speaking. And if Gladys or Charlie were to meet me in the street, they might not be as tactful as you were—because they don't seem to be very happy about my passing for white. I don't see why, though. I'm not hurting them any, and I send you money every week and help out just as much as they do, if not more. Tell them not to queer me, Ma, if they should ever run into me and the girlfriend any place. Maybe it would have been better if you and they had stayed in Cincinnati and I'd come away alone when we decided to move after the old man died. Or at least, we should have gone to different towns, shouldn't we?

Gee, Ma, when I think of how Papa left everything to his white family, and you couldn't legally do anything for us kids, my blood boils. You wouldn't have a chance in a Kentucky court, I know, but maybe if you'd tried anyway, his white children would have paid you something to shut up. Maybe they wouldn't want it known in the papers that they had colored brothers. But you was too proud, wasn't you, Ma? I wouldn't have been so proud.

Well, he did buy you a house and send all us kids through school. I'm glad I finished college in Pittsburgh before he died. It was too bad about Charlie and Gladys having to drop out, but I hope Charlie gets something better to do than working in a garage. And from what you told me in your last letter about Gladys, I don't blame you for being worried about her—wanting to go in the chorus of one of those South Side cabarets. Lord! But I know it's really tough for girls to get any kind of job during this depression, especially for colored girls, even if Gladys is high yellow, and smart. But I hope you can keep her home, and out of those South Side dumps. They're no place for a good girl.

Well, Ma, I will close because I promised to take my weakness to the movies this evening. Isn't she sweet to look at, all blonde and blue-eyed? We're making plans about our house when we get married. We're going to take a little apartment on the North Side, in a good neighborhood, out on one of those nice quiet side streets where there are trees. I will take a box at the post office for your mail. Anyhow, I'm glad there's nothing to stop letters from crossing the color-line. Even if we can't meet often, we can write, can't we, Ma?

With love from your son,

JACK.

■ ■ ■

We Shall Overcome

President Lyndon B. Johnson

*On March 15, 1965, President Johnson gave the following
speech to Congress. It was intended as an introduction to
the Voting Rights Act, which passed shortly afterward. A few
days previously, in Selma, Ala., a civil-rights activist had
been murdered during a peaceful demonstration.*

At times history and fate meet at a single time in a single
place to shape a turning point in man's unending search
for freedom. So it was at Lexington and Concord. So it
was a century ago at Appomattox. So it was last week in
Selma, Alabama. There, long-suffering men and women
peacefully protested the denial of their rights as Americans.
Many were brutally assaulted. One good man, a man of
God, was killed. There is no cause for pride in what has
happened in Selma. There is no cause for self-satisfaction
in the long denial of equal rights of millions of Americans.
But there is cause for hope and for faith in our democracy
in what is happening here tonight.

For the cries of pain and the hymns and protests of
oppressed people have summoned into convocation all
the majesty of this great Government—the Government
of the greatest Nation on earth. Our mission is at once
the oldest and the most basic of this country: to right
wrong, to do justice, to serve man. In our time we have
come to live with moments of great crisis. Our lives have
been marked with debate about great issues; issues of
war and peace, issues of prosperity and depression. But
rarely in any time does an issue lay bare the secret heart

of America itself. Rarely are we met with a challenge, not to our growth or abundance, our welfare or our security, but rather to the values and the purposes and the meaning of our beloved Nation.

The issue of equal rights for American Negroes is such an issue. And should we defeat every enemy, should we double our wealth and conquer the stars, and still be unequal to this issue, then we will have failed as a people and as a nation. For with a country as with a person, "What is a man profited, if he shall gain the whole world, and lose his own soul?"

There is no Negro problem. There is no Southern problem. There is no Northern problem. There is only an American problem. And we are met here tonight as Americans—not as Democrats or Republicans—we are met here as Americans to solve that problem.

THE RIGHT TO VOTE

The most basic right of all [i]s the right to choose your own leaders. The history of this country, in large measure, is the history of the expansion of that right to all of our people.

Many of the issues of civil rights are very complex and most difficult. But about this there can and should be no argument. Every American citizen must have an equal right to vote. There is no reason which can excuse the denial of that right. There is no duty which weighs more heavily on us than the duty we have to ensure that right. Yet the harsh [reality] is that in many places in this country men and women are kept from voting simply because they are Negroes. Every device of which human ingenuity is capable has been used to deny this right. The Negro citizen may go to register only to be told that the day is wrong, or the hour is late, or the official in charge is absent. And if he persists, and if he manages to present himself to the registrar, he may be disqualified because he did not spell out his middle name or because he abbreviated a word on the application. And if he manages to fill out an application he is given a test. The registrar is the sole judge of whether he passes this test. He may be asked to recite the entire Constitution, or explain the most complex provisions of State law. And even a college degree cannot be used to prove that he can read and write.

For the fact is that the only way to pass these barriers is to show a white skin. Experience has clearly shown that the existing process of law cannot overcome systematic and ingenious discrimination. No law that we now have on the books—and I have helped to put three of them there—can ensure the right to vote when local officials are determined to deny it. In such a case our duty must be clear to all of us. The Constitution says that no person shall be kept from voting because of his race or his color. We have all sworn an oath before God to support and to defend that Constitution. We must now act in obedience to that oath.

GUARANTEEING THE RIGHT TO VOTE

This bill will strike down restrictions to voting in all elections—Federal, State, and local—which have been used to deny Negroes the right to vote. This bill will establish a simple, uniform standard which cannot be used, however ingenious the effort, to flout our Constitution. It will provide for citizens to be registered by officials of the United States Government if the State officials refuse to register them. It will eliminate tedious, unnecessary lawsuits which delay the right to vote. Finally, this legislation will ensure that properly registered individuals are not prohibited from voting.

To those who seek to avoid action by their National Government in their own communities; who want to and who seek to maintain purely local control over elections, the answer is simple: Open your polling places to all your people. Allow men and women to register and vote whatever the color of their skin. Extend the rights of citizenship to every citizen of this land.

THE NEED FOR ACTION

There is no constitutional issue here. The command of the Constitution is plain. There is no moral issue. It is wrong—deadly wrong—to deny any of your fellow Americans the right to vote in this country. There is no issue of States rights or national rights. There is only the struggle for human rights. I have not the slightest doubt what will be your answer.

WE SHALL OVERCOME

But even if we pass this bill, the battle will not be over. What happened in Selma is part of a far larger movement which reaches into every section and State of America. It is the effort of American Negroes to secure for themselves the full blessings of American life. Their cause must be our cause too. Because it is not just Negroes, but really it is all of us, who must overcome the crippling legacy of bigotry and injustice. And we shall overcome.

As a man whose roots go deeply into Southern soil I know how agonizing racial feelings are. I know how difficult it is to reshape the attitudes and the structure of our society. But a century has passed, more than a hundred years, since the Negro was freed. And he is not fully free tonight. It was more than a hundred years ago that Abraham Lincoln, a great President of another party, signed the Emancipation Proclamation, but emancipation is a proclamation and not a fact. A century has passed, more than a hundred years, since equality was promised. And yet the Negro is not equal. A century has passed since the day of promise. The time of justice has now come. I tell you that I believe sincerely that no force can hold it back. It is right in the eyes of man and God that it should come. And when it does, I think that day will brighten the lives of every American. For Negroes are not the only victims. How many white children have gone uneducated, how many white families have lived in stark poverty, how many white lives have been scarred by fear, because we have wasted our energy and our substance to maintain the barriers of hatred and terror?

So I say to all of you here, and to all in the Nation tonight, that those who appeal to you to hold on to the past do so at the cost of denying you your future. This great, rich, restless country can offer opportunity and education and hope to all: black and white, North and South, sharecropper and city dweller. These are the enemies: poverty, ignorance, disease. They are the enemies and not our fellow man, not our neighbor. And these enemies too, poverty, disease and ignorance, we shall overcome.

PROGRESS THROUGH THE DEMOCRATIC PROCESS

The real hero of this struggle is the American Negro. His actions and protests, his courage to risk safety and even to risk his life, have awakened the conscience of this Nation. His demonstrations have been designed to call attention to injustice, designed to provoke change, designed to stir reform.

He has called upon us to make good the promise of America. And who among us can say that we would have made the same progress were it not for his persistent bravery, and his faith in American democracy. For at the real heart of battle for equality is a deep seated belief in the democratic process. Equality depends not on the force of arms or tear gas but upon the force of moral right; not on recourse to violence but on respect for law and order.

There have been many pressures upon your President and there will be others as the days come and go. But I pledge you tonight that we intend to fight this battle where it should be fought in the courts, and in the Congress, and in the hearts of men. We must preserve the right of free speech and the right of free assembly. But the right of free speech does not carry with it, as has been said, the right to holler fire in a crowded theater. We must preserve the right to free assembly, but free assembly does not carry with it the right to block public thoroughfares to traffic. We do have a right to protest, and a right to march under conditions that do not infringe the constitutional rights of our neighbors. And I intend to protect all those rights as long as I am permitted to serve in this office. We will guard against violence, knowing it strikes from our hands the very weapons which we seek—progress.

In Selma as elsewhere we seek and pray for peace. We seek order. We seek unity. But we will not accept the peace of stifled rights, or the order imposed by fear, or the unity that stifles protest. For peace cannot be purchased at the cost of liberty. In Selma tonight, as in every [. . .] city, we are working for just and peaceful settlement. We must all remember that after this speech I am making tonight, after the police and the FBI and the Marshals have all gone, and after you have promptly passed this bill, the people of Selma and the other cities of the Nation must still live and work together. And when the attention of the Nation has gone elsewhere they must try to heal the wounds and to build a new community.

This cannot be easily done on a battleground of violence, as the history of the South itself shows. It is in recognition of this that men of both races have shown such an outstandingly impressive responsibility in recent days—last Tuesday, again today.

THE PURPOSE OF THIS GOVERNMENT

My first job after college was as a teacher in Cotulla, Texas, in a small Mexican-American school. Few of them could speak English, and I couldn't speak much Spanish. My students were poor and they often came to class without breakfast, hungry. They knew even in their youth the pain of prejudice. They never seemed to know why people disliked them. But they knew it was so, because I saw it in their eyes. I often walked home late in the afternoon, after the classes were finished, wishing there was more that I could do. But all I knew was to teach them the little that I knew, hoping that it might help them against the hardships that lay ahead.

Somehow you never forget what poverty and hatred can do when you see its scars on the hopeful face of a young child. I never thought then, in 1928, that I would be standing here in 1965. It never even occurred to me in my fondest dreams that I might have the chance to help the sons and daughters of those students and to help people like them all over this country. But now I do have that chance—and I'll let you in on a secret—I mean to use it. And I hope that you will use it with me.

■ ■ ■

After the Revolution
Henry Louis Gates, Jr.

Legendary figures of an era of civil rights—and black power—talk about what went wrong, what went right, and what is to be done.

Angela Davis

A militant African American activist, Davis was tried on charges of kidnapping, murder, and conspiracy connected with an unsuccessful escape and kidnapping attempt of the Soledad (Prison) brothers in 1970. An all-white jury acquitted Davis of the charges.

Racism has undergone some fundamental changes, both structurally and ideologically, which means that we can no longer use the old theories, the old strategies, in order to try to chart our movement forward. I see racism as such being even *more* dangerous in the latter nineties than it was in the fifties and sixties. For one thing, it is more structurally entrenched in the economic system, and so the globalization of capital has led to racist structures that are often not recognized as racism.

I'm one who always warns against the nostalgic identification with the radicalism of the sixties and early seventies. But I think there are lessons that we can learn. Even at the height of the nationalist era, there was a great deal of discussion about the connections between race and class, about the importance of understanding the structural components of racism. There was an understanding that we couldn't assume that racism was just about prejudice—which, unfortunately, is what not only conservatives but liberals are arguing today.

Eldridge Cleaver

Cleaver preached the doctrine of black power, urging blacks to organize politically so that they could deal with white society from a position of strength. He wrote of black attitudes toward American society in his book Soul on Ice *and described his religious conversion in* Soul on Fire. *Cleaver died in 1998.*

. . . In terms of things getting worse, you know, I think we have lost our vision and our purpose. Back in the sixties and fifties, we knew what we were doing: we were struggling, one, to get rid of the remnants of segregation; two, to get rid of political oppression and exclusion; and, three, to get rid of economic oppression and exploitation. The Supreme Court dealt with the segregation issue; then Congress started passing all kinds of voter-rights and civil-rights acts, and so basically one and two were resolved. If you called a meeting today to ask people to come and discuss segregation, nobody would come but Louis Farrakhan, David Duke, and, maybe, Newt Gingrich. If you called a meeting to talk about how we need more black politicians, nobody would come except a bunch of black politicians and wannabes. But if you called a meeting to talk about money you'd have a standing-room-only crowd, and it wouldn't be all black.

The No. 1 need in the black community today is for a coup d'état against our elected representatives,

because our leaders took the only political machinery
that we had, which was protest machinery, and parcelled it out among themselves as political-campaign
machinery. And that left the community voiceless,
unrepresented. All they knew was "Protest, protest,
get me into power." And, once they got into power,
"Protest, protest, keep me in power." That's it.

James Farmer

*Farmer was assistant secretary of the Department of
Health, Education, and Welfare in 1969 and 1970.
He was involved in founding the Congress of Racial
Equality (CORE) and served as its national director.
He also served as program director of the National
Association for the Advancement of Colored People
(NAACP).*

Malcolm and I, in a debate, could say opposite things,
and we'd both get thunderous applause. That was
because the people in the audience were saying, "I'm
not a social engineer, I don't know how to solve these
problems, but you two guys are trying to do it. More
power to you, both of you."

The March on Washington in '63 was the last great
middle-class demonstration. The poor folk were not
there. The followers of Malcolm were not there. But
after the March on Washington the young people in the
inner city, who had been bystanders watching it on TV
up in their slum apartments, said, "Hey, let me take a
look at this." And these were young people who had
rejected the twin foci of the march and of the movement up until that time: nonviolence and interracialism.

The young folk from the inner city were saying, "What is this we-shall-overcome, black-and-white together stuff? I don't know of any white folks except the guy who runs that store on 125th Street in Harlem and garnishees wages and repossesses things you buy. I'd like to go upside his head. Who else do I know? I know the rent collector, who bangs on the door demanding rent that we ain't got. I'd like to go upside *his* head. So there won't be no black and white together." The young people in the street were not only young and angry; they were also illiterate, or largely so, they were unskilled, and they were unemployed and largely unemployable, because of their lack of training, lack of skills, and lack of literacy. The country doesn't realize that Martin Luther King was under attack from the young people in the inner city then. Nonviolence was like a profanity to them.

Most of us thought that if we could wipe out Jim Crow the race problem would be solved. In the sixties, problems were simple. The front seat of a bus, a hot dog at a lunch counter. It was good against evil, right against wrong. Now, sometimes, it's right against right.

Maulana Ron Karenga

In 1966 Dr. Karenga, a black-studies professor at California State University at Long Beach, created Kwanzaa (Swahili: "first fruits") as a celebration of family and social values. By the early 1990s Kwanzaa was estimated to have more than 5 million celebrants.

The movement did not realize how deeply racism was a part of the political culture of America, and how there was not only a racial dimension to oppression but a class dimension, which had to be dealt with. This is how I understand and see this creation of what William Julius Wilson calls this truly disadvantaged crowd: None of the problems we have today are new, except in their exaggerated form. There was dope, there was teenage pregnancy, there was crime, but we were able to hold them at bay because we had an institutional capacity to intervene and prevent them in a timely manner. But here, with the institutional drain, the resource and brain drain caused by the abandonment of the community by a significant segment of the middle class, you don't have that capacity. It's another irony of history that in order to be American in the way that the integrationists defined it you almost had to deny your own identity. The Japanese or the Jews can be Americans and Japanese or Jewish at the same time. But for some reason people push us to choose either one or the other. And what that does is undermine the basis for community: it undermines the basis for an institutional capacity to define, defend, and develop our interests.

The civil-rights discourse was a *moral* discourse based on an appeal to whites to realize their own humanity and act accordingly. The presumption that the people who hold power are moral rather than amoral is the fatal flaw of the movement: it depends so much on the good will of the oppressor and of the white allies you had. On the other hand, the black-power movement's fundamental problem was that it focussed essentially on *power*. We found out that we cannot organize and sustain the organization with just power talk, because we don't have the principles around which to organize. We must now combine the political and the moral.

Kwame Ture
(Formerly Stokely Carmichael)

West Indian–born black nationalist leader Stokely Carmichael joined the SNCC in 1960 and in 1961 was one of the Freedom Riders traveling through the South to oppose segregation in interstate transportation. Carmichael emigrated in Guinea, West Africa, in 1969 and changed his name to Kwame Ture. He died in Guinea in 1998.

The greatest success of the civil-rights movement was raising the level of consciousness about people. Its greatest failure was a lack of organization. When you look at the sixties, the organizations that came to the forefront, like S.N.C.C. and CORE, were incapable of attaching the head and the hands. In the sixties, most of your movement was spontaneous, not organized. This was its greatest weakness. Of course, this weakness can be traced to the fact that those organizations didn't see the need for ideology at that point. Even the Student Nonviolent Coordinating Committee. One of its greatest weaknesses was that it didn't see the need for unifying ideology.

To be quite honest with you, much as I hate American capitalism and fight to destroy it I never thought I would see the conditions that I now see existing in America. The homelessness, the alienation of the people, the right wing turning against the government. While all this is certainly favorable for me, because I'm a revolutionary and I'm gonna work for revolution in America, I really never thought that I would see conditions as backward as they are and as aggravated as they are in America today.

I know my people are ready to fight, and they're conscious. Their consciousness is higher today than it was in the sixties. In every aspect of life in America, the American capitalist system tries to make it appear as if the people were less conscious now than they were in the sixties. Nothing could be further from the truth. You cannot tell me that a woman in the sixties was as much conscious as a woman in the nineties is today. What they took in the sixties a woman in the nineties will never take. We don't even have to talk about the environment issue. Everything in America is becoming politicized, whether it's abortion or busing. So the people in America are more politicized than they were in the sixties, not less.

Integration makes no sense at all—we might as well face that. It's not a question of integration; it's a question of power. People think that racism is a question of attitude. It's not. If I sit on a bus next to a white man, and he doesn't like me sitting next to him, and he has an attitude, that's his problem. But if he has the power to move me from the front of the bus to the back of the bus, then that's *my* problem. The problem of racism arises only when there's power to carry out your acts. That's why when they talk about reverse racism I laugh at them. We have no power. The only way we will get power is when Africa is unified and socialist.

Julian Bond

In 1960 Bond joined in creating the SNCC. When he was first elected to the Georgia House of Representatives, in 1965, the members refused to seat him because of his opposition to U.S. involvement in the Vietnam War. The Supreme Court ruled that he must be seated, and he served for ten years. He helped found, and became the president of, the Southern Poverty Law Center, which works to protect the rights of poor people of all races.

We've lost a great deal of our moral standing. I think we need to try to regain it if we can, but I think we also have to become more clever politically, in the larger sense. The time hasn't quite come when we forget group politics altogether, but we've got to play that politics *and* larger politics, too. To play only one is to lock yourself into a little room from which there is no escape. You have your chieftains and your queens, but that's it. They're presiding over a tiny principality.

Once, we thought that segregation and racism were the same thing, and that, when segregation was done away with, racism would be done away with, too. We enjoyed the community of segregation, and it conflated all the differences among us into one un-differentiated mass. This unfortunate luxury blinded us to the reality of the diversity of our "community," and the prospect that after segregation that diversity would spread and increase. You've had a dispersal of black Americans from this ghetto status that all used to suffer from, and this dispersal has had positive and negative effects. The positive is that now, if you've got the dough, you can live wherever you want to. You can move away from overcrowding and bad police protection and all that, and move wherever you want to. On the negative side, it has destroyed something we tend to romanticize but what really was an organic community with a wide variety of people living in it, up and down the income stream, and where the community imposed a kind of standard of behavior. It wasn't always met, but at least there were models.

■ ■ ■

A Knowing So Deep

Toni Morrison

I think about us, Black women, a lot. How many of us are battered and how many are champions. I note the strides that have replaced the tiptoe; I watch the new configurations we have given to personal relationships, wonder what shapes are forged and what merely bent. I think about the sisters no longer with us, who, in rage or contentment, left us to finish what should never have begun: a gender/racial war in which everybody would lose, if we lost, and in which everybody would win, if we won. I think about the Black women who never landed who are still swimming open-eyed in the sea. I think about those of us who did land and see how their strategies for survival became our maneuvers for power.

I know the achievements of the past are staggering in their everydayness as well as their singularity. I know the work undone is equally staggering, for it is nothing less than to alter the world in each of its parts: the distribution of money, the management of resources, the way families are nurtured, the way work is accomplished and valued, the penetration of the network that connects these parts. If each hour of every day brings fresh reasons to weep, the same hour is full of cause for congratulations: Our scholarship illuminates our past, our political astuteness brightens our future, and the ties that bind us to other women are in constant repair in order to build strength in this present, now.

I think about us, women and girls, and I want to say something worth saying to a daughter, a friend, a mother, a sister—my self. And if I were to try, it might go like this:

Dear Us: You were the rim of the world—its beginning. Primary. In the first shadow the new sun threw, you carried inside you all there was of startled and startling life. And you were there to do it when the things of the world needed words. Before you were named, you were already naming.

Hell's twins, slavery and silence, came later. Still you were like no other. Not because you suffered more or longer, but because of what you knew and did before, during, and following that suffering. No one knew your weight until you left them to carry their own. But you knew. You said, "Excuse me, am I in the way?" knowing all the while that you were the way. You had this canny ability to shape an untenable reality, mold it, sing it, reduce it to its manageable, transforming essence, which is a knowing so deep it's like a secret. In your silence, enforced or chosen, lay not only eloquence but discourse so devastating that "civilization" could not risk engaging in it lest it lose the ground it stomped. All claims to prescience disintegrate when and where that discourse takes place. When you say "No" or "Yes" or "This and not that," change itself changes.

So the literature you live and write asks and gives no quarter. When you sculpt or paint, organize or refute, manage, teach, nourish, investigate or love, you do not blink. Your gaze, so lovingly unforgiving, stills, agitates, and stills again. Wild or serene, vulnerable or steel trap, you are the touchstone by which all that is human can be measured. Porch or horizon, your sweep is grand.

You are what fashion tries to be—original and endlessly refreshing. Say what they like on Channel X, you are the news of the day. What doesn't love you has trivialized itself and must answer for that. And anybody who does not know your history doesn't know their own and must answer for that too.

You did all right, girl. Then, at the first naming, and now at the renaming. You did all right. You took the hands of the children and danced with them. You defended men who could not defend you. You turned grandparents over on their sides to freshen sheets and white pillows. You made meals from leavings, and leaving you was never a real separation because nobody needed your face to remember you by. And all along the way you had the best of company—others, we others, just like you. When you cried, I did too. When we fought, I was afraid you would break your fingernails or split a seam at the armhole of your jacket. And you made me laugh so hard the sound of it disappeared—returned, I guess, to its beginning when laughter and tears were sisters too.

There is movement in the shadow of a sun that is old now. There, just there. Coming from the rim of the world. A disturbing disturbance that is not a hawk nor stormy weather, but a dark woman, of all things. My sister, my me—rustling, like life.

1985

■ ■ ■

The Saint

V. S. Pritchett

When I was seventeen years old I lost my religious faith.
It had been unsteady for some time and then, very suddenly, it went as the result of an incident in a punt on the
river outside the town where we lived. My uncle, with
whom I was obliged to stay for long periods of my life,
had started a small furniture-making business in the town.
He was always in difficulties about money, but he was
convinced that in some way God would help him. And
this happened. An investor arrived who belonged to a
sect called the Church of the Last Purification, of Toronto,
Canada. Could we imagine, this man asked, a good and
omnipotent God allowing his children to be short of
money? We had to admit we could not imagine this.
The man paid some capital into my uncle's business and
we were converted. Our family were the first Purifiers—
as they were called—in the town. Soon a congregation
of fifty or more were meeting every Sunday in a room
at the Corn Exchange.

At once we found ourselves isolated and hated people. Everyone made jokes about us. We had to stand
together because we were sometimes dragged into the
courts. What the unconverted could not forgive in us
was first that we believed in successful prayer and, sec-
ondly, that our revelation came from Toronto. The success of our prayers had a simple foundation. We regarded
it as 'Error'—our name for Evil—to believe the evidence
of our senses, and if we had influenza or consumption,
or had lost our money or were unemployed, we denied

the reality of these things, saying that since God could not
have made them they therefore did not exist. It was ex-
hilarating to look at our congregation and know that what
the vulgar would call miracles were performed among
us, almost as a matter of routine, every day. Not very big
miracles, perhaps; but up in London and out in Toronto,
we knew that deafness and blindness, cancer and insan-
ity, the great scourges, were constantly vanishing before
the prayers of the more advanced Purifiers.

'What!' said my school master, an Irishman with eyes
like broken glass and a sniff of irritability in the bristles
of his nose. 'What! Do you have the impudence to tell
me that if you fell off the top floor of this building and
smashed your head in, you would say you hadn't fallen
and weren't injured?'

I was a small boy and very afraid of everybody, but
not when it was a question of my religion. I was used to
the kind of conundrum the Irishman had set. It was useless to argue, though our religion had already developed
an interesting casuistry.

'I *would* say so,' I replied with coldness and some
vanity. 'And my head would not be smashed.'

'You would not say so,' answered the Irishman. 'You
would not say so.' His eyes sparkled with pure pleasure.
'You'd be dead.'

The boys laughed, but they looked at me with
admiration.

Then, I do not know how or why, I began to see a
difficulty. Without warning and as if I had gone into my
bedroom at night and had found a gross ape seated in
my bed and thereafter following me about with his
grunts and his fleas and a look, relentless and ancient,

scored on his brown face, I was faced with the problem
which prowls at the centre of all religious faith. I was
faced by the difficulty of the origin of evil. Evil was an
illusion, we were taught. But even illusions have an origin. The Purifiers denied this.

I consulted my uncle. Trade was bad at the time and
this made his faith abrupt. He frowned as I spoke.

'When did you brush your coat last?' he said. 'You're
getting slovenly about your appearance. If you spent more
time studying books'—that is to say, the Purification
literature—'and less with your hands in your pockets
and playing about with boats on the river, you wouldn't
be letting Error in.'

All dogmas have their jargon; my uncle as a business
man loved the trade terms of the Purification. 'Don't let
Error in,' was a favourite one. The whole point about the
Purification, he said, was that it was scientific and therefore exact; in consequence it was sheer weakness to admit
discussion. Indeed, betrayal. He unpinched his pince-nez,
stirred his tea and indicated I must submit or change the
subject. Preferably the latter. I saw, to my alarm, that my
arguments had defeated my uncle. Faith and doubt
pulled like strings round my throat.

'You don't mean to say you don't believe that what
our Lord said was true?' my aunt asked nervously, following me out of the room. 'Your uncle does, dear.'

I could not answer. I went out of the house and down
the main street to the river where the punts were stuck like
insects in the summery flash of the reach. Life was a dream,
I thought; no, a nightmare, for the ape was beside me.

I was still in this state, half sulking and half exalted,
when Mr Hubert Timberlake came to the town. He was

one of the important people from the headquarters of
our Church and he had come to give an address on the
Purification at the Corn Exchange. Posters announcing this
were everywhere. Mr Timberlake was to spend Sunday
afternoon with us. It was unbelievable that a man so emi-
nent would actually sit in our dining-room, use our knives
and forks, and eat our food. Every imperfection in our home
and our characters would jump out at him. The Truth had
been revealed to man with scientific accuracy—an accuracy we could all test by experiment—and the future course
of human development on earth was laid down, finally. And
here in Mr Timberlake was a man who had not merely performed many miracles—even, it was said with proper
reserve, having twice raised the dead—but who had
actually been to Toronto, our headquarters, where this
great and revolutionary revelation had first been given.

'This is my nephew,' my uncle said, introducing me.
'He lives with us. He thinks he thinks, Mr Timberlake, but
I tell him he only thinks he does. Ha, ha.' My uncle was
a humorous man when he was with the great. 'He's
always on the river,' my uncle continued. 'I tell him he's
got water on the brain. I've been telling Mr Timberlake
about you, my boy.'

A hand as soft as the best quality chamois leather took
mine. I saw a wide upright man in a double-breasted navy
blue suit. He had a pink square head with very small ears
and one of those torpid, enamelled smiles which were
said by our enemies to be too common in our sect.

'Why, isn't that just fine?' said Mr Timberlake, who,
owing to his contacts with Toronto, spoke with an
American accent. 'What say we tell your uncle it's funny
he thinks he's funny.'

The eyes of Mr Timberlake were direct and colourless. He had the look of a retired merchant captain who had become decontaminated from the sea and had reformed and made money. His defence of me had made me his at once. My doubts vanished. Whatever Mr Timberlake believed must be true and as I listened to him at lunch, I thought there could be no finer life than his.

'I expect Mr Timberlake's tired after his address,' said my aunt.

'Tired?' exclaimed my uncle, brilliant with indignation. 'How can Mr Timberlake be tired? Don't let Error in!'

For in our faith the merely inconvenient was just as illusory as a great catastrophe would have been, if you wished to be strict, and Mr Timberlake's presence made us very strict.

I noticed then that, after their broad smiles, Mr Timberlake's lips had the habit of setting into a long depressed sarcastic curve.

'I guess,' he drawled, 'I guess the Al-mighty must have been tired sometimes, for it says He re-laxed on the seventh day. Say, do you know what I'd like to do this afternoon,' he said, turning to me. 'While your uncle and aunt are sleeping off this meal let's you and me go on the river and get water on the brain. I'll show you how to punt.'

Mr Timberlake, I saw to my disappointment, was out to show he understood the young. I saw he was planning a 'quiet talk' with me about my problems.

'There are too many people on the river on Sundays,' said my uncle uneasily.

'Oh, I like a crowd,' said Mr Timberlake, giving my uncle a tough look. 'This is the day of rest, you know.' He had had my uncle gobbling up every bit of gossip from the sacred city of Toronto all the morning.

My uncle and aunt were incredulous that a man like Mr Timberlake should go out among the blazers and gramophones of the river on a Sunday afternoon. In any other member of our Church they would have thought this sinful.

'Waal, what say?' said Mr Timberlake. I could only murmur.

'That's fixed,' said Mr Timberlake. And on came the smile as simple, vivid and unanswerable as the smile on an advertisement. 'Isn't that just fine!'

Mr Timberlake went upstairs to wash his hands. My uncle was deeply offended and shocked, but he could say nothing. He unpinched his glasses.

'A very wonderful man,' he said. 'So human,' he apologised.

'My boy,' my uncle said. 'This is going to be an experience for you. Hubert Timberlake was making a thousand a year in the insurance business ten years ago. Then he heard of the Purification. He threw everything up, just like that. He gave up his job and took up the work. It was a struggle, he told me so himself this morning. "Many's the time," he said to me this morning, "when I wondered where my next meal was coming from." But the way was shown. He came down from Worcester to London and in two years he was making fifteen hundred a year out of his practice.

To heal the sick by prayer according to the tenets of the Church of the Last Purification was Mr Timberlake's profession.

My uncle lowered his eyes. With his glasses off the lids were small and uneasy. He lowered his voice too.

'I have told him about your little trouble,' my uncle said quietly with emotion. I was burned with shame. My uncle looked up and stuck out his chin confidently.

'He just smiled,' my uncle said. 'That's all.'

Then we waited for Mr Timberlake to come down.

I put on white flannels and soon I was walking down to the river with Mr Timberlake. I felt that I was going with him under false pretences; for he would begin explaining to me the origin of evil and I would have to pretend politely that he was converting me when, already, at the first sight of him, I had believed. A stone bridge, whose two arches were like an owlish pair of eyes gazing up the reach, was close to the landing-stage. I thought what a pity it was the flannelled men and the sunburned girls there did not know I was getting a ticket for *the* Mr Timberlake who had been speaking in the town that very morning. I looked round for him and when I saw him I was a little startled. He was standing at the edge of the water looking at it with an expression of empty incomprehension. Among the white crowds his air of brisk efficiency had dulled. He looked middle-aged, out of place and, insignificant. But the smile switched on when he saw me.

'Ready?' he called. 'Fine!'

I had the feeling that inside him there must be a gramophone record going round and round, stopping at that word.

He stepped into the punt and took charge.

'Now I just want you to paddle us over to the far bank,' he said, 'and then I'll show you how to punt.'

Everything Mr Timberlake said still seemed unreal to me. The fact that he was sitting in a punt, of all common-place material things, was incredible. That he should propose to pole us up the river was terrifying. Suppose he fell into the river. At once I checked the thought. A leader of our Church under the direct guidance of God could not possibly fall into a river.

The stream is wide and deep in this reach, but on the southern bank there is a manageable depth and a hard bottom. Over the clay banks the willows hang, making their basket-work print of sun and shadow on the water, while under the gliding boats lie cloudy, chloride caverns. The hoop-like branches of the trees bend down until their tips touch the water like fingers making musical sounds. Ahead in midstream, on a day sunny as this one was, there is a path of strong light which is hard to look at unless you half close your eyes, and down this path on the crowded Sundays, go the launches with their parasols and their pennants; and also the rowing boats with their beetle-leg oars, which seem to dig the sunlight out of the water as they rise. Upstream one goes, on and on between the gardens and then between fields kept for grazing. On the afternoon when Mr Timberlake and I went out to settle the question of the origin of evil, the meadows were packed densely with buttercups.

'Now,' said Mr Timberlake decisively when I had paddled to the other side. 'Now I'll take her.'

He got over the seat into the well at the stern.

'I'll just get you clear of the trees,' I said.

'Give me the pole,' said Mr Timberlake, standing up on the little platform and making a squeak with his boots as he did so. 'Thank you, sir. I haven't done this for eighteen years, but I can tell you, brother, in those days I was considered some poler.'

He looked around and let the pole slide down through his hands. Then he gave the first difficult push. The punt rocked pleasantly and we moved forward. I sat facing him, paddle in hand, to check any inward drift of the punt.

'How's that, you guys?' said Mr Timberlake looking round at our eddies and drawing in the pole. The delightful water swished down it.

'Fine,' I said. Deferentially I had caught the word.

He went on to his second and third strokes, taking too much water on his sleeve, perhaps, and uncertain in his steering, which I corrected, but he was doing well.

'It comes back to me,' he said. 'How am I doing?'

'Just keep her out from the trees,' I said.

'The trees?' he said.

'The willows,' I said.

'I'll do it now,' he said. 'How's that? Not quite enough? Well, how's this?'

'Another one,' I said. 'The current runs strong this side.'

'What? More trees?' he said. He was getting hot.

'We can shoot out past them,' I said. 'I'll ease us over with the paddle.'

Mr Timberlake did not like this suggestion.

'No, don't do that. I can manage it,' he said. I did not want to offend one of the leaders of our Church, so I put the paddle down; but I felt I ought to have taken him farther along away from the irritation of the trees.

'Of course,' I said. 'We could go under them. It might be nice.'

'I think,' said Mr Timberlake, 'that would be a very good idea.'

He lunged hard on the pole and took us towards the next archway of willow branches.

'We may have to duck a bit, that's all,' I said.

'Oh, I can push the branches up,' said Mr Timberlake.

'It is better to duck,' I said.

We were gliding now quickly towards the arch, in fact I was already under it.

'I think I should duck,' I said. 'Just bend down for this one.'

'What makes the trees lean over the water like this?' asked Mr Timberlake. 'Weeping willows—I'll give you a thought there. How Error likes to make us dwell on sorrow. Why not call them *laughing* willows?' discoursed Mr Timberlake as the branch passed over my head.

'Duck,' I said.

'Where? I don't see them,' said Mr Timberlake turning around.

'No, your head,' I said. 'The branch,' I called.

'Oh, the branch. This one?' said Mr Timberlake finding a branch against his chest and he put out a hand to lift it. It is not easy to lift a willow branch and Mr Timberlake was surprised. He stepped back as it gently and firmly leaned against him. He leaned back and pushed from his feet. And he pushed too far. The boat went on, I saw Mr Timberlake's boots leave the stern as he took an unthoughtful step backwards. He made a last minute grasp at a stronger and higher branch, and then there he hung a yard above the water, round as a blue damson that is ripe and ready, waiting only for a touch

to make it fall. Too late with the paddle and shot ahead
by the force of his thrust, I could not save him.

For a full minute I did not believe what I saw; indeed
our religion taught us never to believe what we saw.
Unbelieving I could not move. I gaped. The impossible
had happened. Only a miracle, I found myself saying,
could save him.

What was most striking was the silence of Mr Timberlake
as he hung from the tree. I was lost between gazing at
him and trying to get the punt out of the small branches
of the tree. By the time I had got the punt out, there
were several yards of water between us, and the soles of
his boots were very near the water as the branch bent
under his weight. Boats were passing at the time but no
one seemed to notice us. I was glad about this. This was
a private agony. A double chin had appeared on the face
of Mr Timberlake and his head was squeezed between
his shoulders and his hanging arms. I saw him blink and
look up at the sky. His eyelids were pale like a chicken's.
He was tidy and dignified as he hung there, the hat was
not displaced and the top button of his coat was done
up. He had a blue silk handkerchief in his breast pocket.
So unperturbed and genteel he seemed that as the tips
of his shoes came nearer and nearer to the water, I became alarmed. He could perform what are called miracles. He would be thinking at this moment that only in
an erroneous and illusory sense was he hanging from the
branch of the tree over six feet of water. He was probably praying one of the closely reasoned prayers of our
faith, which were more like conversations with Euclid
than appeals to God. The calm of his face suggested
this. Was he, I asked myself, within sight of the main

road, the town Recreation Ground, and the landing-
stage crowded with people, was he about to re-enact a
well-known miracle? I hoped that he was not. I prayed
that he was not. I prayed with all my will that Mr Timberlake
would not walk upon the water. It was my prayer and
not his that was answered.

I saw the shoes dip, the water rise above his ankles
and up his socks. He tried to move his grip to a yet
higher branch—he did not succeed—and in making
this effort his coat and waistcoat rose and parted from
his trousers. One seam of shirt with its pant-loops and
brace-tabs broke like a crack across the middle of Mr
Timberlake. It was like a fatal flaw in a statue, an earth-
quake crack which made the monumental mortal. The
last Greeks must have felt as I felt then, when they saw
a crack across the middle of some statue of Apollo. It
was at this moment I realised that the final revelation
about man and society on earth had come to nobody
and that Mr Timberlake knew nothing at all about the
origin of evil.

All this takes long to describe, but it happened in a
few seconds as I paddled towards him. I was too late to
get his feet on the boat and the only thing to do was to
let him sink until his hands were nearer the level of the
punt and then to get him to change hand-holds. Then
I would paddle him ashore. I did this. Amputated by
the water, first a torso, then a bust, then a mere head
and shoulders, Mr Timberlake, I noticed, looked sad
and lonely as he sank. He was a declining dogma. As the
water lapped his collar—for he hesitated to let go of the
branch to hold the punt—I saw a small triangle of dep-
recation and pathos between his nose and the corners of

his mouth. The head resting on the platter of water had the sneer of calamity on it, such as one sees in the pictures of a beheaded saint.

'Hold on to the punt, Mr Timberlake,' I said urgently. 'Hold on to the punt.'

He did so.

'Push from behind,' he directed in a dry business-like voice. They were his first words. I obeyed him. Carefully I paddled him towards the bank. He turned and, with a splash, climbed ashore. There he stood, raising his arms and looking at the water running down his swollen suit and making a puddle at his feet.

'Say,' said Mr Timberlake coldly, 'we let some Error in that time.'

How much he must have hated our family.

'I am sorry, Mr Timberlake,' I said. 'I am most awfully sorry. I should have paddled. It was my fault. I'll get you home at once. Let me wring out your coat and waistcoat. You'll catch your death . . .'

I stopped. I had nearly blasphemed. I had nearly suggested that Mr Timberlake had fallen into the water and that to a man of his age this might be dangerous.

Mr Timberlake corrected me. His voice was impersonal, addressing the laws of human existence, rather than myself.

'If God made water it would be ridiculous to suggest He made it capable of harming his creatures. Wouldn't it?'

'Yes,' I murmured hypocritically.

'OK,' said Mr Timberlake. 'Let's go.'

'I'll soon get you across,' I said.

'No,' he said. 'I mean let's go on. We're not going to let a little thing like this spoil a beautiful afternoon.

Where were we going? You spoke of a pretty landing-place farther on. Let's go there.'

'But I must take you home. You can't sit there soaked to the skin. It will spoil your clothes.'

'Now, now,' said Mr Timberlake. 'Do as I say. Go on.'

There was nothing to be done with him. I held the punt into the bank and he stepped in. He sat like a bursting and sodden bolster in front of me while I paddled. We had lost the pole of course.

For a long time I could hardly look at Mr Timberlake. He was taking the line that nothing had happened and this put me at a disadvantage. I knew something considerable had happened. That glaze, which so many of the members of our sect had on their faces and persons, their minds and manners, had been washed off. There was no gleam for me from Mr Timberlake.

'What's the house over there?' he asked. He was making conversation. I had steered into the middle of the river to get him into the strong sun. I saw steam rise from him.

I took courage and studied him. He was a man, I realised, in poor physical condition, unexercised and sedentary. Now the gleam had left him one saw the veined empurpled skin of the stoutish man with a poor heart. I remembered he had said at lunch:

'A young woman I know said, "Isn't it wonderful. I can walk thirty miles in a day without being in the least tired." I said, "I don't see that bodily indulgence is anything a member of the Church of the Last Purification should boast about."'

Yes, there was something flaccid, passive, and slack about Mr Timberlake. Bunched and swollen clothes, he refused to take them off. It occurred to me, as he looked with boredom at the water, the passing boats, and the country, that he had not been in the country before. That it was something he had agreed to do but wanted to get over quickly. He was totally uninterested. By his questions— what is that church? Are there any fish in this river? Is that a wireless or a gramophone?—I understood that Mr Timberlake was formally acknowledging a world he did not live in. It was too interesting, too eventful a world. His spirit, inert and preoccupied, was elsewhere in an eventless and immaterial habitation. He was a dull man, duller than any man I have ever known; but his dullness was a sort of earthly deposit left by a being whose diluted mind was far away in the effervescence of metaphysical matters. There was a slightly pettish look on his face as (to himself, of course) he declared he was not wet and he would not have a heart attack or catch pneumonia.

Mr Timberlake spoke little. Sometimes he squeezed water out of his sleeve. He shivered a little. He watched his steam. I had planned, when we set out, to go up as far as the lock, but now the thought of another two miles of this responsibility was too much. I pretended I wanted to go only as far as the bend which we were approaching, where one of the richest buttercup meadows was. I mentioned this to him. He turned and looked with boredom at the field. Slowly we came to the bank.

We tied up the punt and we landed.

'Fine,' said Mr Timberlake. He stood at the edge of the meadow just as he had stood at the landing-stage— lost, stupefied, uncomprehending.

'Nice to stretch our legs,' I said. I led the way into the deep flowers. So dense were the buttercups there was hardly any green. Presently I sat down. Mr Timberlake looked at me and sat down also. Then I turned to him with a last try at persuasion. Respectability, I was sure, was his trouble.

'No one will see us,' I said. 'This is out of sight of the river. Take off your coat and trousers and wring them out.'

Mr Timberlake replied firmly:

'I am satisfied to remain as I am.'

'What is this flower?' he asked to change the subject.

'Buttercup,' I said.

'Of course,' he replied.

I could do nothing with him. I lay down full length in the sun; and, observing this and thinking to please me, Mr Timberlake did the same. He must have supposed that this was what I had come out in the boat to do. It was only human. He had come out with me, I saw, to show me that he was only human.

But as we lay there I saw the steam still rising. I had had enough.

'A bit hot,' I said getting up.

He got up at once.

'Do you want to sit in the shade,' he asked politely.

'No,' I said. 'Would you like to?'

'No,' he said. 'I was thinking of you.'

'Let's go back,' I said. We both stood up and I let him pass in front of me. When I looked at him again I stopped dead. Mr Timberlake was no longer a man in a navy blue suit. He was blue no longer. He was trans- figured. He was yellow. He was covered with buttercup pollen, a fine yellow paste of it made by the damp, from head to foot.

'Your suit,' I said.

He looked at it. He raised his thin eyebrows a little, but he did not smile or make any comment.

The man is a saint, I thought. As saintly as any of those gold-leaf figures in the churches of Sicily. Golden he sat in the punt; golden he sat for the next hour as I paddled him down the river. Golden and bored. Golden as we landed at the town and as we walked up the street back to my uncle's house. There he refused to change his clothes or to sit by a fire. He kept an eye on the time for his train back to London. By no word did he acknowledge the disasters or the beauties of the world. If they were printed upon him, they were printed upon a husk.

Sixteen years have passed since I dropped Mr Timberlake in the river and since the sight of his pant loops destroyed my faith. I have not seen him since, and today I heard that he was dead. He was fifty-seven. His mother, a very old lady with whom he had lived all his life, went into his bedroom when he was getting ready for church and found him lying on the floor in his shirt-sleeves. A stiff collar with the tie half inserted was in one hand. Five minutes before, she told the doctor, she had been speaking to him.

The doctor, who looked at the heavy body lying on the single bed, saw a middle-aged man, wide rather than stout and with an extraordinarily box-like thick-jawed face. He had got fat, my uncle told me, in later years. The heavy liver-coloured cheeks were like the chaps of a hound. Heart disease, it was plain, was the cause of the death of Mr Timberlake. In death the face was lax, even coarse and degenerate. It was a miracle, the doctor said, that he had lived as long. Any time during the last twenty years the smallest shock might have killed him.

I thought of our afternoon on the river. I thought of him hanging from the tree. I thought of him, indifferent and golden in the meadow. I understood why he had made for himself a protective, sedentary blandness, an automatic smile, a collection of phrases. He kept them on like the coat after his ducking. And I understood why—though I had feared it all the time we were on the river—I understood why he did not talk to me about the origin of evil. He was honest. The ape was with us. The ape that merely followed me was already inside Mr Timberlake eating out his heart.

■ ■ ■

James Baldwin
(1924–1987)

Although the power of racial conflict and the power of
love eventually became James Baldwin's central themes,
it was through the power of the *word* that he first made
his mark in the world. Born and raised in New York City,
Baldwin—at the age of fourteen—became a preacher
at the Fireside Pentecostal Assembly in Harlem, the
'Little Minister' who excited and mesmerized congrega-
tions. Rhythm and cadence, rhetoric and intellect, the
ability to convey fierce conviction verbally—the hall-
marks of his life as a mature writer—evolved from his
life as a boy preacher.

Older, established writers helped Baldwin discover
his talent and decide on his profession. At Frederick
Douglass Junior High School, he joined the literary
club and received valuable direction from the club's
advisor, Countee Cullen, the renowned poet of the
Harlem Renaissance. At De Witt Clinton High School in
the Bronx, Baldwin became an editor of *The Magpie,*
the school literary magazine, to which he contributed
stories, poems, and plays. Living in Greenwich Village
in the 1940s, Baldwin also met the novelist Richard
Wright, the famous author of *Native Son.* Wright, who
had been his idol, gave the young man both encour-
agement and practical help, recommending him for a
fellowship and putting him in touch with a publisher.
In later years, however, Baldwin came to realize that
he and Wright were different kinds of writers, and their
friendship dissolved.

Baldwin's first novel, *Go Tell It on the Mountain,* was published in 1953 and received much critical acclaim. As he continued to forge his career, Baldwin lived part of the time in France, and eventually he would spend most of his time there. Through the 1950s and 1960s, he combined his gift for narrative and his fiery social conscience in a series of well-crafted works in a variety of forms, including the novel *Another Country,* the essays in *Nobody Knows My Name: More Notes of a Native Son,* and the plays *The Amen Corner* and *Blues for Mr. Charlie.*

Although he saw his role as primarily that of an intellectual and a writer, Baldwin did not hesitate to take direct action in the civil rights movement. He addressed radio and television audiences and gave numerous speeches, including one at the 1961 Congress of Racial Equality (CORE) rally in Washington, D.C. Upon his return from a tour of Africa, Baldwin gave talks and interviews throughout the South, and in May 1963 he led a group of civil rights activists in a meeting with Attorney General Robert Kennedy.

Baldwin's work for civil rights was both large-scale and small-scale: In August of the volatile year 1963, he took part in the massive March on Washington, and in October he helped to register black voters in Selma, Alabama. He marched from Selma to Montgomery in 1965 with Dr. Martin Luther King Jr., and he attended King's funeral in 1968. Throughout this time, during which he was appearing on the dangerous front lines of the civil rights struggle, Baldwin continued to write intense essays and stories. In fact, Baldwin's writing often seems to derive much of its power from his ability to blend the personal and the public, the private and the political.

In 1971, Baldwin bought a large house in St. Paul-de-Vence, France, where he frequently received guests from around the world: writers, intellectuals, activists, entertainers. He occasionally visited the United States to attend meetings, give interviews, and teach college courses at such schools as the University of California at Berkeley, Bowling Green College in Ohio, and the University of Massachusetts at Amherst. Despite attempts to balance a relentless schedule, he was hospitalized for exhaustion in 1984.

Baldwin's collected nonfiction, *The Price of the Ticket,* was published in 1985, and in 1986 he was named an officer of the French Legion of Honor. On December 1, 1987, at his home in St. Paul-de-Vence, James Baldwin died of cancer of the esophagus. At a funeral service in New York, the novelist Toni Morrison and the poets Maya Angelou and Amiri Baraka gave heartfelt eulogies of the brilliant man they knew as a world-class intellectual, an African American leader, an artist, and a loving friend.

■ ■ ■